Is Making Heavy Water Painful?

Stanley M. Davies

First edition March, 2023

Self-published on Amazon.ca

ISBN: 9798377591016

CONTENTS

ACKNOWLEDGMENTS

Friends and family for pre-reading the manuscript

Cover foreground pictures: Stanley Davies
Cover background picture: Ray Davies
Cover graphics: Ralph Saulnier

FORWARD

In the late sixties, a strange and enormous structure began to arise outside the little town of Port Hawkesbury, Nova Scotia. It towered over the pulp mill, which had been operating for several years, and even dwarfed the neighboring power plant, which was being built to serve it. The words 'Heavy Water' entered the vocabulary of the populace for the first time.

The project was huge, novel and dangerous. The towers being built at Point Tupper were the largest pressure vessels in North America, and would hold 600 tons of potentially lethal hydrogen sulphide. The production process itself, while modelled on a working and proven design, was a tenfold scale-up in size. Water pumps, gas compressors, and heat exchangers were commensurately large. The laboratory equipment was state of the art and was being used right up to its limits. And then, almost as an afterthought, came the managers, engineers, technicians, maintenance workers and operators who would make the whole thing run.

The people came from all over the world. PhD's from Czechoslovakia worked alongside kids straight out of local schools. Autocratic managers from Upper Canada came face to face with stubborn Cape Breton union leaders. Experienced supervisors from Alberta and New Brunswick were given operators who had to be taught how a heat exchanger worked. Housing in boomtown Port Hawkesbury was almost unobtainable, and forty mile drives to work in the often foul Cape Breton weather were commonplace. And once at work, you had to be careful. Despite what you may have been taught at school about the 'rotten eggs gas', one sniff can kill you, and you won't smell a thing. And then, as though all that wasn't enough, the process didn't work properly, and it took five years of struggle, strikes, experiments and modifications to get the plant up to full production, with corporate presidents, vice-presidents, and various politicians breathing down your neck all the time. I loved every minute of it!

I spent seven years in Cape Breton, Nova Scotia, working to first commission, and later to bring to full production, the Canadian General Electric Heavy Water plant at Point Tupper. This was, for Canada, a pivotal and crucial project. The CANDU line of nuclear power plants was beginning to make its mark in the world. Ontario Hydro had made a major commitment to the technology, and CANDU plants were being sold abroad in successful competition with American companies. But, in contrast to the American designs,

CANDU needed a plentiful, secure and inexpensive source of heavy water. Atomic Energy of Canada had already scoured the world, and had let one contract for heavy water production to Deuterium Corporation of America. Their plant was being built at Glace Bay, Cape Breton, but was rumored to be in trouble. It used a novel process, and was extremely late coming into production. Atomic Energy of Canada had requested Canadian General Electric to build a second plant.

It was also a unique time for southern Cape Breton. A novel, high-tech, dangerous industry was to be dumped in their back yard, but jobs were so desperately needed that it was accepted, more or less uncomplainingly. Challenges abounded for native and newcomer alike, but people being people, and particularly, Cape Bretoners being Cape Bretoners, the challenge was more often met with acceptance, humor, and even enthusiasm, rather than with fear, despair, or resignation. I intend to write a book which conveys the excitement and, yes, fun of engineering on the enormous scale we practiced. The book will be factual and anecdotal, with the focus on the people and the humor of the day-to-day happenings. The technology will be woven in to supplement the content, and to provide a background. The stories are variously poignant, funny, sad, and, thankfully rarely, tragic. Readers will absorb some simple science, and hopefully get a feel for what drives an engineer.

There are a few books on the history of Canada's Nuclear Program. For example, *Nucleus, the History of Atomic Energy of Canada Limited* by Robert Bothwell, was published in 1988. This book and others like it are, if you will excuse the phrase, as dry as dust, being written for technical and historical readers. Most of the seventeen pages on heavy water discuss the politics and failures of the Deuterium of Canada heavy water plant at Glace Bay. Canadian General Electric is mentioned briefly, Port Hawkesbury not at all.

ABOUT THE AUTHOR

I am a physicist, mutated by the pressure of earning a living into an engineer, and later a mid-level corporate manager. I hold an Honors Degree from Kings College, London University. Born in 1932, I was raised and educated in England. I am now a naturalized citizen of the United States, retired in San Jose, California. I emigrated from England to Canada in 1966 and from Canada to the USA in 1975.

I have worked on guided missiles, nuclear power plants for both terrestrial and space applications, and in chemical operations. The events related in this book occurred between 1968 and 1975, while I was working for Canadian General Electric at their heavy water plant in southern Cape Breton. I held a variety of management positions, but was principally responsible for the production of the process, and for the process modifications which finally resulted in the plant reaching its design capability in 1974.

I come from a literary family; my sister has published several books relating to history, poetry and literature. I have written and/or edited numerous extensive technical reports, many over 1000 pages, but my efforts to introduce humor did not receive upper management approval.

Now, I have been able to let myself go with this, writing what I hope is an entertaining, yet factual, account of the problems people face in bringing a large and dangerous chemical plant into full production.

1 MEETINGS

Dundee has a spectacular scenic location at the south end of the Bras D'Or Lakes, on Cape Breton Island, Nova Scotia. Today it is the site of a world class golf resort; in the spring of 1969 it was a sleepy little hamlet, typical of many which can still be found in that part of the world, basking in the sun, or sleeping under its mantle of snow. Joy and Stan Davies drove slowly through the winding lanes that spring morning in 1969, seeking the site of the company picnic. A pair of drowsy dogs in a driveway sensed an alien presence approaching. As the car neared, they roused themselves, and began a curious circling manoeuver. Slowly chasing their own tails, they accelerated their rotation as the car passed, and, like stones slung from a pair of invisible sling shots, they chased the car down the road as they barked wildly. Duty done and intruders banished, they returned, scratched contentedly, and, like the little community itself, resumed an interrupted sleep.

Stan had come to Cape Breton to take a new job with Canadian General Electric. A physicist by training, but rapidly mutating into an engineer under the sheer pressure of earning a living, he possessed a lively and inquisitive mind, which did not always work in a predictable logical manner. He found unexpected cross-connections in many things. These cross-connections were frequently humorous, to him at least. He was not afraid; indeed, he positively reveled in the new, the novel, the untested, and the untried. Of average build, a pair of twinkling bright blue eyes peered out of an unprepossessing face from under a shock of prematurely greying hair. His wife, Joyce, was several inches shorter, a brunette, attractive, vivacious, with well-shaped legs and a nicely proportioned figure, although beginning to labor against the extra pounds which had not entirely left her since the birth of the twins 10 years ago. She had left school early, and struggled constantly with the idea that she was inferior to her husband and his friends because of her lack of education. But she possessed a great fund of common sense, which was invaluable in tempering her husband's wilder flights of fancy, and in compensating for his notorious absentmindedness, which seemed to affect everything except his work.

A crudely hand-drawn cardboard sign pointed to the spectacularly beautiful site at which the picnic was already starting. To the north of the road, a small beach fronted on the sparkling waters of West Bay, with Marble Mountain glinting a majestic white in the distance. To the south, a field sloped up towards Sporting Mountain, its vivid emerald green contrasting startlingly with the sky blue waters of the Bras D'Or Lakes stretching to the east. Not long out from England, the peculiarly North American institution of the company picnic was a novelty to Joy and Stan. At the top of a knoll sat a few trestle tables, and twenty or thirty people milled about, some already attacking the coolers filled with beer and sodas. More supplies arrived every minute from the constantly growing number of cars and trucks parked on the road below.

Don Nazzer, the plant manager, presided. Tall, thin, somewhat taciturn, and autocratic, Don was the consummate corporate professional. Normally aloof, and hard to get to know, he maintained his distance from his subordinates. "If you do your job, I'll stay out of your way." seemed to be his guiding principal. Stan's mind went back to a surprise birthday party, recently thrown for Don by his staff, and obviously a surprise to Don. "I must be treating you guys too good," he was heard to mutter. Today, Don relaxed sufficiently to greet the arriving newcomers cordially, if not effusively. Stan offered to help get things set up, and in the best spirit of corporate delegation, was handed off to Len.

Len Nordby, the engineering manager, greeted his new help with, for him, enthusiasm. He was a solid, stocky individual, very much his own man, and the epitome of a Canadian engineer. Thorough, hardworking, knowledgeable, unemotional, and not afraid to take a prudent risk, he was as much in charge of this event as he was in charge of plant engineering. Sending Joy to help with the food, he asked Stan to help organize a tug of war. With his inborn reserve,

Stan was appalled, but British to the last, kept a stiff upper lip and concealed his apprehension. He had not expected to start his Port Hawkesbury management career by press ganging these salaried, or worse, hourly paid, employees into the corporate idea of a good time. His mind whirled as he walked over to the box Len had pointed out. "Would bribery, threats or intimidation be best?" he thought. But no sooner was the rope laid out, than people flocked around. With no regard for position, expertise, social station or income, but with much horsing around and rough and ready humor, two approximately equal teams organized themselves. They took up positions on each side of the two lines drawn in the grass... the symbolism of which seemed lost on everyone except himself. Stan gravely intoned, "Take up the strain." and the rope tightened. Tying his handkerchief to the middle of the rope, he shouted, "Pull!" and the game began. Inexorably, the white marker moved left as the weaker team struggled and slipped to stop their slide to defeat. As the handkerchief crossed the winner's line, Stan called, "Gerry's team wins!" and everyone collapsed on the grass, huffing and laughing. Stan was elated. He wondered, "Was this all it took to build real team spirit in this astounding country? Was it really this easy?" He was ready to go again... who knows, this time he could really show commitment to democratic values by pulling on a team, not just adjudicating. But it was not to be.

Gerry Harley was on the winning team, and Dave King was watching. In the Port Hawkesbury melting pot, they had already formed a firm friendship. Gerry was one of the shift supervisors, hired from western Canada. Tall, handsome, and muscular, to anybody familiar with motor cycles, his name portrayed his character, solid and dependable. Gerry was a scuba diver, and was an expert in resuscitation techniques. He exuded the rawboned confidence of Canada. Dave was also a shift supervisor, of slight build, but sharp intellect. He came from a New Brunswick oil refinery. He liked to question Stan on science and how the process worked, often cornering him about some point of engineering knowledge on which Stan was not too sure. "That's the trouble with you engineers," Dave once said, "On one hand, this. On the other hand, that. Why don't you just keep one hand in your pocket?"

As the teams paused to get a drink and catch their breath, Gerry relaxed and surveyed the wondrous scenery. "This sure was pretty, he thought. "Not majestic, like his native Alberta with the Canadian Rockies rising as a backdrop to the monotonous plains, but scenic. The lake, the ocean, the beaches... not a bad part of the world to make a life. Have to get some diving and fishing in. That beach down there, now..." and his stomach gave a familiar lurch. "Oh, no. Not again. Not another." With a shout, Gerry rushed down the hill, bounded across the road, and plunged waste deep into the icy water. Reaching the inert figure floating face down, he dragged him back to the shore. Finding no pulse or breathing, he began the classic resuscitation routine. One, two, three, pounds over the heart, and then one full expansion of the lungs, in a gesture of unreserved human affection, with his mouth covering the victims lips. "God, the breath was foul." he thought. "His prostrate victim had been drinking all day by the smell of it. He closed his mind to the vile sensory stimuli of the body beneath him. One, two, three, breathe; one, two, three, breathe. Just like the last time. Only then the victim had been his buddy, incautiously removing his gas mask around a leaking well, and the H_2S had got him. One minute a living, laughing friend, the next a lifeless lump of meat. But I got him back," Gerry thought savagely, "and I can get this one back too."

Dave was next to arrive and took over the heart massage. Soon a crowd gathered round, all watching helplessly as the drama played out on that brightly sunlit beach. The victim had been identified, and his wife, pushed to the front, watched the scene without a flicker of emotion. "Was she hoping he was gone?" Gerry wondered. "What would marriage be like to a man drunk by noon?"

A volunteer was dispatched to find a doctor, but how quickly could a doctor be expected to arrive on a remote Cape Breton beach, on a Saturday afternoon? Gerry and Dave knew they were on their own, with a life dependent on their ministrations. Dave took a rest from his pounding and checked the inert figure's pulse, "At least the heart's restarted." he pronounced, prompting a little sigh to pass through the crowd. The mouth to mouth resuscitation was organized on a rotating basis.

"Thank God for that." Gerry muttered. After about 15 minutes, the victim began to breathe on his own, but still did not regain consciousness. Don raged about the lack of medical services in this part of Cape Breton, while others began to talk quietly among themselves.

Eventually a tall, thin, taciturn individual appeared, claiming to be a doctor. "More like the grim reaper, than an angel of mercy," thought Stan to himself. The doctor appraised the scene unemotionally, took the victim's pulse, looked at his eyeball reflex, listened to his heart, and stood up. "You say you found him in the water?" he asked. "How long had he been there?"

"I'm not sure," Gerry replied, "but I think only a short time."

"Have you checked his lungs for water?" was the next question. It hung in the air and there was an uneasy silence.

"How do you do that?" everyone seemed to be thinking. Gerry cursed inwardly, "Of course, this was a drowning, not a gassing."

"Right." said the doctor, "You two strong lads there, lift him up by his heels and hang him head down!"

This rough and ready approach to medicine was too much for a formal Upper Canadian, and Don stepped forward. "Excuse me sir," he said, "are you a licensed physician?"

The doctor looked at him coldly. "Of course I am. How many drowning cases have you dealt with?" he asked.

Don retreated, suitably chastened. The victim was hung by his heels for a few seconds, and much to everybody's relief no gush of water emerged from his mouth. His color, however, did seem to improve, helped no doubt by the rush of blood to the head. "I think he's just sleeping it off." Gerry whispered to Stan.

The ambulance still did not show. Finally, they improvised. The victim was deposited on an old sleeping bag in somebody's station wagon, and dispatched to the Antigonish hospital, a drive of about 50 miles. With the star attraction gone, the company picnic was not able to survive; personnel relationships were just too new and fragile to be sustained in such a traumatic event. Nobody was in the mood for revelry; most of the food went uneaten; the children's favors were unused; even the drinks went undrunk, a great rarity in Cape Breton. To Stan's overwrought imagination, an unspoken accusation hung in the air, "We don't know whose fault it was," and he could hear people thinking, "but if you folks hadn't been here, this wouldn't have happened." The victim turned up at work a few days later, seeming none the worse for the experience. He claimed it was so hot, he had just waded in the water to cool off, and remembered nothing else.

So the first attempt by the Canadian General Electric management team to find common ground with the employees of their new Cape Breton Heavy Water plant ended ignominiously. The culture gap between the Upper Canadians on one side, and the locally hired workers on the other, was huge, and was to plague both labor and management for years to come. The management and professional staff embodied all the desirable corporate traits: self-motivated, industrious, hardworking and innovative. One and all, they had been lured to remote Cape Breton by promotions, generous salaries, and the prospects of advancement that came with starting up a new corporate enterprise. The local labor had much in common with the coal mining culture from the north end of the island. They were self-reliant, proud, independent, and brave when necessary, but always suspicious of management motives. Stan was often to wonder in the years following the picnic, how different things might have been if that first attempt at togetherness had succeeded.

Port Hawkesbury, 20 miles south of Dundee, was the center of most activities, although 'the plant', as it soon came to be called by all, was actually outside the town, outside the county, and indeed, often seemed to be outside the world, and in a different universe. Port Hawkesbury was originally the port for the ferry to Cape Breton from Mulgrave, on the mainland side of the Strait of Canso. The strait ran almost due northwest-southeast for over 10 miles, and was a scenic splendor in its own right. In the 1950's, a causeway had been built by the simple expedient of blasting out the side of a nearby mountain and bulldozing it into the strait. The resulting causeway terminated at Port Hastings, an even smaller town about 2 miles northwest of Port Hawkesbury, and carried a road, a railway line, and a power line. Before the construction of the causeway, the strait was frequently blocked by huge quantities of drift ice, floating down from the partly fresh and thus more easily frozen, waters of the Gulf of St. Lawrence. This passage was now blocked, and as a result, Port Hawkesbury found itself in a magnificent, sheltered, deep water harbor, ripe for development. Port Hawkesbury was, by a quirk of cartographic fate, just inside the county line of Inverness, which stretched to the north and west. The industrial area was Point Tupper, just southeast down the strait, in the county of Richmond. Point Tupper already had a gypsum mine, a shipyard, and a pulp mill. Now, in addition to Canadian General Electric's heavy water plant, Nova Scotia Power was building a 150 megawatt electric power plant, and Gulf Oil was constructing a refinery and deep water supertanker terminal. It was all too much for the infrastructure of the little town to absorb. Moreover, the tax revenues from these industries, $150,000 per year for Canadian General Electric's plant alone, went to Arichat, the capital of Richmond County, and not to Port Hawkesbury, which was to struggle under an insufficient tax base for years.

To find a place to live in Port Hawkesbury in 1968 was almost impossible. Most of the construction workers came from all over Cape Breton and northern Nova Scotia, either driving up to a hundred miles a day, or bedding down in dreary construction camps of trailers. The lucky few employees who had been hired first had snapped up the smattering of new and existing homes that were up for sale; others had parked trailers on the sites of future construction. The town was busting at the seams, stores bustling, the bowling alley and curling rink always crowded, and of course always long lines at the provincial liquor store.

Canadian General Electric, which, for brevity, will be referred to as CGE from now on, had acquired one large, nicely located, four bedroom house, right in the center of town, for the temporary use of its employees seeking housing. Both Gerry and Stan stayed there in the autumn of 1968. The house was looked after by the local CGE housing manager, Anabelle. Anabelle was one of the eternal earth mothers of this world, glorying in the simple pleasures of looking after people. A large, cheery, statuesque woman, she could not do enough to please. The problem was that she specialized in Cape Breton construction cooking, and Gerry, Stan and the other residents began to balloon. At that time, if you took lunch in the construction camp cafeteria, as you walked down the line, you would typically be asked two questions, "How many steaks?" and, "How many tea bags?" Genuine Cape Breton tea was a real education for a delicate English lad. The pot of tea would be made first thing in the morning, kept on the stove to simmer, and periodically replenished with water and tea bags. By mid-day, one sip would curl your eyebrows!

Waiting for the plant to be completed, entertainment and recreation was a problem. Small social groups began to form around common interests. Such was the genesis of the poker group, which did much to keep its adherents sane through the next seven years. And such was the genesis of the famous duck à l'orange dinner. A tradition had formed at the company house that if you were there over the weekend, i.e. if you were not home on a connubial visit, Saturday night dinner would be provided, in turns, by one of the residents. Colin and his wife, Roberta, happened to be residents at the time. Colin was an English maintenance engineer who had probably come to Canada late in life to seek his fortune, but things had not quite worked out as expected. He had spent several years at an iron ore plant in Labrador; to hear him and his wife talk, Cape Breton was paradise by comparison. Roberta had recently opened Port Hawkesbury's first book store, and was trying hard to introduce some British culture into Canadian life. And so when Colin announced he had linked up with a group going duck hunting, leaving very early Saturday, expecting to be home soon after mid-day, Roberta came alive. "I have an excellent recipe for duck à l'orange," she announced gaily, "and that's our dinner for tonight. It will be a change from steak." Gerry and Stan were delighted. It would indeed be a change from steak, but more importantly, it relieved them of the cooking duty. Next morning, Roberta was out shopping early. About 4 pm the vultures began to gather. Roberta was devastated - no Colin had appeared. Consoling themselves, and Roberta, with the cocktails, hors d'oeuvres and wine, ribald jokes began to circulate about Colin's probable location. Roberta participated manfully, but her dreams of an elegant dinner party were fading fast. About 6 pm Colin showed up. Obviously feeling no pain, since the duck hunting party, like any other Cape Breton collective recreational activity, had been provided with a generous measure of alcoholic beverages. He produced two scraggly feathered bundles. Roberta set to work, but no culinary art could rescue these birds. Everything else about the dinner was perfect - the wine, the vegetables and the sauce. The duck was so tough that it was almost inedible. Gerry maintained privately to Stan that they were sea-gulls!

The several new employees from Alberta were, of course, entranced with the ocean. Stan, born in a seaside town, was happy to be back in his native habitat. And so, soon came the natural question, "How do we go fishing?" The locals began to divulge their secret streams and creeks, but that was not good enough for Gerry, "I mean real deep sea fishing, not this freshwater stuff."

Going to sea for fun was a novel thought to most Cape Bretoners. For some, it was a cold, wet, dangerous necessity. But, through the good offices of Anabelle, a deal was finally struck. Prospective fishermen were to report to the Mulgrave dock, with the appropriate liquid refreshment for ourselves and our captain, who would supply the boat and the gear. And so it came to pass that about a dozen people, including four women, found themselves on a flat decked, diesel powered, Cape Cod style tug, chugging out into the Strait of Canso with little fuss but much smoke and soot. It was a glorious summer day and the liquor soon broke the ice. Soon the boat cut its engine to drift silently in the middle of the strait. The neophytes learned they were to go 'jigging', a new experience for all. The gear was broken out. It comprised a number of 100 yard lengths of stout cord, to the bottom of which, at intervals of about 18 inches, were attached a number of shiny stainless steel weights, triangular in cross section. Each weight sported a fearsome looking, three-pronged curved hook at the bottom. There was no bait.

"It works like this," said our captain, scotch and water in hand. "You drop the gear over the side until it touches the bottom. The water's about 280 feet deep here, so you'll need most of that line. Then you haul it up about three to six feet, and begin to jig, like this." He illustrated with slow rhythmic sweeps of his arm. "Then the fish see this flashing thing in the water, and swim over to have a look. And then you've got 'em!"

Gerry and Stan looked at one another. "It's going to be a long day," said Stan philosophically, and broke open another beer to make it shorter.

Soon, with all the lines over the side, jigging began in earnest, with no result whatsoever. The liquid refreshment began to disappear faster, and murmurs of revolt were heard. "Do you think he's having us on? I've never seen fishing without any bait. How does he know there are any fish here?"

The captain sensed the impatience, and said, "Here, hang on a bit, I'll move the boat to a better spot." The would-be fishermen watched in unbelief as he started the engine and moved a few hundred yards up the strait. "There, try that," the captain said. Stan was not about to be spoofed again, and opened another beer while some of his more credulous companions dropped their lines over the side and again resumed their rhythmic jerking.

"Hey, I think I've got something!" came a surprised shout. Soon it was joined by others. Fish were caught by every part of their anatomy, mentionable as well as unmentionable, in the flank, in the tail, through the cheek. The captain, scotch and water still in his hand, appraised each catch as it was hauled it in, advising which was good eating, and which should be thrown back. Later that day, a happy band of adventurers straggled ashore. The captain would take no money. The drinks we provided, and a share of the catch, was all that he wanted. The resulting fish fry that night, all agreed, beat Duck a l'Orange into a cocked hat.

The new people who would make the plant run kept coming. Len had hired Peter Roxon; a second or third generation Polish Canadian as his chief engineer. Like his boss, Peter was a solid mechanical engineer, who could soon recite the performance statistics of every pump, compressor, and valve in the plant. Like his boss, he was thorough to a fault. His buxom wife, Margarete, was French

Canadian, and was the life and soul of every party. She maintained to the scandalized locals that Peter would frequently chase her round the bedroom. Looking at them both, the mind would boggle at the thought. Len had also recruited Otto Kveton, a Czechoslovakian, and his attractive wife, Helen. They had escaped when the Russians over-ran their country in the late 1950's. They were both professionally qualified, he as a mechanical engineer, and she as a chemist. Dave Rodgers was also hired for the project. He and his wife, Jane, were two of the few who were actually born in Canada. From New Brunswick, they were a cheerful couple, great fun to be with, always with a joke or funny story to enliven an otherwise dull event. Jane maintained that her first priority every morning was to run the cold water tap to ascertain the color of that day's water supply. Based on that color, she decided to wash or to shop.

Stan had also been doing his share of hiring. Doug Mobley was a young engineer, just finishing the CGE engineer-in-training program, in which recent graduates got to work for a few months in different engineering disciplines. Doug was the son of a Canadian Armed Forces officer who moved frequently, and he had attended 12 schools in as many years. But it obviously had not affected his capabilities, as he was actually that rarity, an engineering physicist. Stan hired him for his computer capabilities, knowing that a theoretical model of the plant performance would soon be needed. Stan also managed to find a local chemist, Leo King. Leo was tall, thin and dark, with a lovely Cape Breton accent. A mark of a true Cape Bretoner was their pronunciation of "three", which always came out of Leo as, "t'ree". Leo maintained to the end that he was hired only as a token Cape Breton professional. Little did he know that Stan was delighted to avoid relocation costs for a professional from Ontario.

And then there was Mark, who Stan had hired to run the laboratory. At that time, Stan thought all the laboratory operations would be routine, using methods developed elsewhere. All he needed was a stickler for detail, who could be relied on to train the locals in precision repetitive measurements. Mark was a stocky, lugubrious, Pole who, as a teenager, had been caught between the advancing Germans and Russians in 1939. He apparently crossed both front lines more than once, finishing on the Russian side when Germany declared war on Russia. He then managed to get himself expatriated, with a bunch of fighting Poles, into Egypt, and ended up finishing his education in English military schools in Egypt and Italy, and finally at a technical college in England. His English pronunciation was good, but his vocabulary was limited. He was certainly a stickler for details, and seemed to hero worship Stan with devotion. Mark could never prevent himself from jumping to attention whenever Stan came in, and seemed to only barely able to suppress the urge to salute. Mark insisted on calling Stan 'sir' if any of the young laboratory technicians were present... and often when they weren't.

And so employees continued to come, from all over the world. Everybody seemed to find housing somewhere. Don had a glorious property at West Arichat, on Isle Madame, about 15 miles due east of the plant as the crow flies, but a good thirty mile drive by road, including the causeway and swing bridge which linked Isle Madame to Cape Breton. While staying in the company house, Stan had been trying desperately to find accommodation for his family, being shown one tumbledown property in which the running water was a hand pump over the sink. He did not think his wife would appreciate that modern convenience. But finally he located a marvelous house, at D'Escousse, also on Isle Madame. The property was owned by the Roman Catholic Church, and had housed the Sisters who taught at the local school. But a brand new school in Arichat made their continued residence there unnecessary. The house was a magnificent, five bedroom, two bathroom structure, about 80 years old, nicely modernized, with oil-fired central heating, its own shared well, and a very modern lightning protection system. Stan thought the latter showed a decided lack of faith on the part of the previous inhabitants, but kept his thoughts to himself. It sat between the road and the beach on a beautiful little sheltered bay. Barely 100 yards away was the local fisherman's jetty. The house was sat sideways to the road, because when it was built the old road ran past its front door. Now it faced a rather dilapidated garage, run by the Poirier brothers. The arrival in the village of a well-to-do family (that is, someone holding a regular job with an Upper Canadian company) caused quite a stir in the little community, but the local inhabitants, both French and English speaking, were very welcoming and neighborly.

Claude Poirier, in particular, went out of his way to make the newcomers feel at home. Claude lived across the road from the garage with his wife and three small children. The house was small and rather dilapidated in Stan's view, but quite typical of many in the village. His job at the garage was bodywork, while his brother, Russel, was a mechanic. Determined to make friends, and realizing from their early contacts that Claude and the newcomers had little in common, he finally asked Stan and Joy if they would like to go for a cruise on his boat. The children had already made their own friends, so one peaceful Sunday afternoon, Stan and Joy accepted. Only later did they come to realize that Claude was a frustrated sailor; he spent his life repairing cars, but his heart was at sea. They joined him on what seemed, on closer inspection, a rather down-at-heel Cape Cod fishing boat. He was in the process of 'restoring' it, as they later found out, a process renewed every two or three years with a different boat. Claude started up the old Ford engine, under the forecastle and chugged slowly out into picturesque Lennox Passage, separating Isle Madame from Cape Breton. Claude steered by the simple expedient of standing looking over the forecastle, with his foot on the rudder cable, gesturing expansively as he showed us the local landmarks. He asked if his guests would like something to drink, and produced an opened bottle of Seven Up. Joy took a swig and almost choked, rum and seven-up, light on the seven-up, being the standard Cape Breton fishing cocktail. The bottle took its place on the forecastle next to Claude. A subsequent expansive gesture up-ended it over the spark plugs! With a few expressive coughs and grunts, the engine spluttered and died, leaving the little party drifting peacefully on the calm waters. Claude, more upset by the loss of his cocktail than by the loss of his engine, made a couple of unsuccessful attempts to restart it. "Now what?" Stan asked.

"Oh, it'll dry out soon." Claude replied. "I'd better check the bilges while we're waiting." He produced a 12 foot long pole with a large leather washer on the end, and thrust it into a pipe on the deck. Working it vigorously up and down, with copious revolting sucking sounds, scummy water began to flow generously up onto the deck and out through the scuppers. Joy, a passable swimmer, who hated cold water, eyed the flow nervously,

"What if the engine doesn't start?" she whispered. But she need not have worried. 'Mucking about in boats' is as much a Cape Breton tradition as it is in England, and after Claude got the engine restarted, they spent the afternoon fishing.

All the Cape Bretoners were friendly, generous to a fault, and eager to make the newcomers at home. You never had to worry if your car broke down on the road... almost inevitably the first car along would stop to see if you needed help. You almost didn't need a car as hitch-hiking was endemic, and rarely did you have to lift your thumb. Of course, driving on the highway you had to be careful. Coming over the brow of hill, or round a bend in the road, you were quite likely to find two cars, stopped opposite each other, drivers with windows down, having a friendly conversation. It was impolite to hoot; in short order the conversation would finish and motoring could resume.

The Cape Bretoners were also eager to draw the newcomers into the life of the community. At election time, about one hour before the polls closed, Stan and Joy began to receive a trickle of visitors. "Yes," said Claude, "there's only the Samson family and poor Mrs. LeBlanc left to vote. Course, she's not been very well, and the Samson's went to town. They should be back soon. Going to vote, are you?" Everybody voted in Cape Breton. Joy and Stan pleaded ignorance of local issues and politicians, but in vain, and their standing in the community diminished somewhat when it became clear they had not voted. Of course, Stan liked to blame this antisocial behavior on the absence of the traditional incentive of a bottle of rum, but since he never disclosed his party allegiance, the rum was never forthcoming.

The children were instantly at home, and in their own way were also drawn into community life. The sense of property ownership had been strongly inculcated in them by their parents, as a way of teaching them to care for their own, as well as others, property. It was not universally shared on the Island. "Where's your bike?" Stan asked one of his twin girls.

She looked uncomfortable, "I lent it to Sheila."

"Where does Sheila live?"

"Somewhere out by West Arichat."

"Hadn't you better get it back?"

"Well, she lent it to Caron to get home." Caron probably lived halfway round the 25 square mile island. But not to worry, a few days later the bike was back, somewhat muddy and obviously well used, returned by neither Sheila nor Caron, but by some fourth or fifth hand who had temporarily acquired it.

In the late 1960's, Isle Madame was still blessed with a manual telephone exchange. The phone was hand cranked, and many lines were party lines: one ring for you and two rings for your compatriot. The exchange was operated out of a private house by an elderly lady, who ate, drank, and slept with her switch board. This inevitably had both advantages and drawbacks. When Stan's eldest daughter called home one day to leave a message for her mother, "Arichat," came the laconic reply over the earpiece.

"Mrs. Davies on extension 38, please." requested a naïve Marion.

"I'm afraid she's not in." replied the disembodied voice. Marion was taken aback.

"I just wanted to leave a message." she said, expecting to be put through immediately.

"Oh, I expect she's gone to chat with Mimi Terrio. Shall I call that number?"

Now Marion's natural English stubbornness came out, "Look, just ring 38, will you?"

"But, I've told you. Mrs. Davies isn't there."

"I'll leave a message with my sister," Marion raged. "Now please put me through". Amid a hurt silence, she was finally connected.

Stan and Joy, living in a homey, if isolated, Cape Breton village, were at least putting down roots and making local contacts. This was not so easy for many of the Upper Canadian and Albertan management and supervisory staff. Living mostly in Port Hawkesbury, the newcomers tended to associate with each other. Don and Len recognized the lack of contact, and despite the picnic fiasco, resolved to try again. This time, being fall, and with plant commissioning about to begin, the mechanism was to be a Friday night dance. The only possible location in Port Hawkesbury was the basement of the Roman Catholic Church. The women's auxiliary was to provide food, and a bar would be set up, with a limited number of complimentary drinks for all. The dance appeared to be quite a success. The various forms of popular rock had operated on Cape Breton folk music to produce a sort of universal rhythmic pulsing sound. The resultant 'dance' was called the Cape Breton stomp. Stan had recently read *The Naked Ape* by Desmond Morris, chronicling his latest theories of human anthropology. His thesis was that man had emerged from the jungle relatively recently, in terms of the human lifetime, and it was therefore not surprising that the human animal retained many characteristics in common with apes. Watching the throbbing mass on the dance floor, waving arms and hips rhythmically, Stan had to conclude that Morris was right.

At the dance, Stan came across Gerard MacMaster, one of the more promising youngsters recently recruited as an hourly paid laboratory technician. He was obviously somewhat under the influence and was horrified that his boss should see him in that condition, no doubt fearing he would be fired on the spot. "Honest, Mr. Davies," he blurted, eyes bulging from a combination of alcohol and earnestness, "I won't do it again. Honest!" Gerard was later promoted to salaried status, and became one of the plant's most reliable and accurate technicians. But Stan doubted he would keep his promise.

The problems began next morning. Stan got up early to go to the bathroom, and had a mild attack of diarrhea, which he put down to an excess of draught beer. An hour later, Joy suffered the same fate, and Stan kidded her about over-imbibing, which she strenuously denied. Then Stan had a second, more severe attack, and began to realize something was wrong. Soon Don called to enquire about his family's health; almost everybody at the dance had been afflicted. For Stan, that remained the only time in his life he had ever hung up on his boss. "Sorry, Don, I've got to go." he gasped as his bowels gave another warning rumble. Communication eventually restored, Don told him the potato salad was suspect. CGE was making arrangements through the plant doctor and local pharmacies to distribute a remedy. Would they like some? You bet they would! Thank goodness the plant was not yet in operation, as it would have been difficult to muster a morning shift.

The little community gloried in the various tales of the social's aftermath for several days. Probably the favorite was of poor George, on his way that Saturday morning to Sydney in his new (second hand) Cadillac, "I just exploded." he maintained. And so the second attempt of locals and newcomers to get to know each other, while more encouraging than the first, could hardly be called a roaring success, unless you like puns. Although later CGE social events in Port Hawkesbury were more successful, the early attempts were certainly dogged by bad luck.

Thankfully, none of the employees knew then that bad luck was to dog the plant for many years. But a new urgency was entering their life. Construction was coming to a close, and some of the plant systems were almost ready to be turned over to those who would maintain and operate them.

2 YOU'RE BUILDING WHAT?

Gerry Harley could not get over the sheer size of the plant. There were eight enormous structures lined up, parallel to the strait. Viewed from the road which ran alongside the plant, and starting from the south east, the tallest was the flare tower. It looked like a miniature 'Tour Eiffel', soaring 450 feet into the sky from a spidery framework. Next were the three identical first stage towers, each 250 feet high and 28 feet in diameter. Then the second stage tower, slightly shorter and slimmer, followed by the two third stage towers, almost as tall but only 12 feet in diameter. Finally, the elevator, which disgorged onto a series of catwalks, joined each tower horizontally. Gerry was used to large chemical complexes; in Alberta they would often cover many acres in an interlocking network of vessels, pipes, and tanks. But these towers were huge, the biggest pressure vessels in North America, so he had been told. He felt somewhat awed, but also grimly determined. Soon these towers would be all his, for eight hours a day.

Gerry listened carefully when Stan explained to a layman why so big. "Well, you see, we don't really make heavy water, we extract it. Right there, in that glass of beer you're drinking, assuming it's made with good Atlantic Canadian water, there is almost 150 parts per million of heavy water. The process we use can extract less than 20% of that, so for every million gallons of fresh water going through our plant, we hope to get almost 20% of 150, or a bit less than 30 gallons of product. The plant is designed to produce about 10 gallons of heavy water per hour, so we will have to process about a third of a million gallons per hour of raw water."

"Actually, rather more than that," thought Gerry, since there were other uses for the water, such as cooling, drinking, sanitary, flushing, etc. With the plant running at full bore, it would use almost 10,000 gallons per minute, the flow from a small river.

The next question was almost invariably, "Just what is heavy water anyway?" to which Stan also had a stock reply. "You remember the molecule of ordinary water is H2O, or two atoms of hydrogen joined to one atom of oxygen. Heavy water has two atoms of deuterium joined to one atom of oxygen. Deuterium is a gas just like hydrogen, except it weighs twice as much. It is called an 'isotope' of hydrogen, from the Greek 'iso', meaning 'the same', and 'tope' meaning 'place'. Literally it is in the same place in the periodic table, and behaves chemically just like hydrogen. Relatively, if a hydrogen atom weighs one unit, deuterium weighs two and oxygen weighs 16. So water, H_2O, weighs 18 units, while heavy water, D_2O, weighs 20. Heavy water, volume for volume, is about 10% heavier than ordinary water".

By this time, the layman's eyes would begin to glaze over. Quantitative thinking did not come easily to most people, Gerry noticed, especially in this remote corner of Canada, and the conversation would soon shift to the relative merits of Moosehead versus Labatts beer, the chances of the Canadiens in that year's Stanley Cup, or some equally erudite topic.

In the short time he had been in Cape Breton, Gerry thought he had seen more rain than in his entire life. If there was one thing the plant would never lack, it was water. He knew the total annual precipitation was over 70 inches per year. His first winter had been a so-called 'open' winter, in which there almost no snow and the lakes barely froze. He could not believe a Canadian winter could be so mild, almost warm in prairie terms. Apparently, it all depended on the track of the great anticyclones which came rolling up the east coast of North America. This year, they had passed to the east, out to sea, the clockwise circulating wind coming in from the south east, relatively warm, but drenched with Gulf Stream moisture. The locals told him to wait for a real Cape Breton winter, but he found it hard to imagine. "What would thirty degrees of frost be like with that wind blowing? And how would the plant stand up to it?" He asked Stan why the plant was built in Cape Breton.

"Well," said Stan, "The most heavy water is found in ocean water, and progressively less is found as you proceed inland. Rain clouds are just water which has been evaporated from the sea by the sun. Like the sea, these clouds contain both light and heavy water. Then, as the clouds move over the land, they drop their water as rain. Naturally, they tend to drop the heavier water first! And that's why these heavy water plants are being built in the Maritimes."

"You're pulling my leg." said Gerry in disbelief.

"No, really!" grinned Stan. "The physics is a bit more complicated, but that's essentially what happens. And that's the official answer, according to the President of CGE. Mind you, there's got to be more to it than just the heavy water concentration. Aren't steam and electricity pretty cheap out west?"

"You bet!" said Gerry with feeling. "Have you seen what we pay for our utility bill out here? I can't believe it".

"Yeah," mused Stan, "and we're going to be using a million pounds per hour of steam, and about 25 Megawatts of electricity. That's going to cost money. Now admittedly, we've got that co-generation deal with Nova Scotia Power. That will reduce our cost of power, but they're oil fired, and oil is imported into Atlantic Canada, so we're going to have to pay for that. The power would have been cheaper out west, even if the feedwater did contain less deuterium. I think CGE was induced to build here by FADIA".

"Who's she when she's awake?" yawned Gerry.

"Federal Area Development Incentive Act. CGE got a $5 million direct grant, no federal or provincial sales tax on production equipment, and a special rapid depreciation allowance against taxes."

"I guess it's as good a use for tax-payer money as any," said Gerry, "The unemployment and poverty around here are pretty bad." Stan certainly had to agree with that sentiment.

"But remember," concluded Stan, "The $50 million, or whatever it costs to build this thing, is CGE's. There's no direct government money; it's all private. In fact, this will be the first heavy water anywhere in the world produced by private money. And CGE only gets its investment back by selling the product to Atomic Energy of Canada. So, we're really on the hook. This thing had better work right!"

Construction proceeded apace. Construction work in Cape Breton paid very well, and was much sought after. If you weren't in the union, you didn't stand a chance. By and large, the labor agreements seemed to hold up. Unofficial strikes were frequent, over real or imagined grievances, but were usually settled relatively quickly. A strike for the first few days of the fall hunting season was a tradition.

Most Cape Bretoners were extremely self-sufficient and independent. Many of them had built their own houses, on lots deeded to them by their parents, and had no mortgage payments. Hunting and fishing could sustain a family for many days, if necessary. This construction work was fine, but it would not last forever, and it was best not to get too excited over it.

The construction supervisors, mostly non-local, were constantly bemoaning the productivity of the local tradesmen. "Good grief", a carpenter supervisor raged, "Do you know what I found one of them doing yesterday? Straightening bent nails, by God. Don't they know I can buy a hundred new nails for what I pay them to straighten one?" The trouble was, 'they' did not think like that. If you are working on your home, and you bend a nail, the store may be 50 miles away.

Cape Bretoners were long accustomed to making do with what they had. The sheer profligacy and urgency of construction on this scale was foreign to them.

Of great concern to Gerry was construction quality. The towers and equipment were to contain 600 tons of an extremely poisonous gas, hydrogen sulphide, or H_2S. Gerry found it hard to imagine the hazard that represented. Out west, most of the natural gas was 'sour', meaning that it was contaminated with H_2S, making it very dangerous. That was why Gerry was here; his experience with H_2S had gotten him a shift supervisor's position at once. However, out west they didn't really use H_2S in large quantities. The natural gas was 'sweetened' as it came out of the ground by separating the H_2S. Then the H_2S was disposed of almost immediately, by converting it to other useful chemicals such as sulphur and sulfuric acid, or by burning it at the top of a flare tower. Soon he would be charged with the safe handling of 600 tons of the stuff!

Gerry had to admit though that there were no short cuts on quality. The construction of the towers themselves was a marvel. The towers were built up of 'courses'. Each course was a cylindrical section 8 feet high. The steel plate, 2 inches thick, arrived from the factory already rolled to the right curvature. Several such plates were welded together on the ground to form the circular course, which was then lifted onto the tower, positioned over the previous course, and welded to form the constantly growing tower. Each plate had been ultrasonically inspected at the factory for flaws. Each weld was inspected in the field by X-ray; any suspect regions were ground or cut out and re-welded. The towers were manufactured under a sub-contract with a specialized manufacturer, and they brought in their own skilled craft labor. There were, however, large pipes, some up to 54 inches in diameter, which were welded into the process by local craftsmen. There were miles of pipe and thousands of welds.

The quest for quality was not always understood by the locals. Stan had told Gerry about a neighbor in D'Escousse with a son, aged about 18, who had recently graduated from trade school as a welder. She wanted Stan to get him a job at the plant; patronage was rife in Nova Scotia. In vain, he did explain that graduation from trade school was not sufficient. Most of the welders at the plant had years of experience, and had to take frequent qualification tests to prove the steadiness of their hand and the quality of their weld. A fairly demanding apprenticeship period was required before you could be considered for a pressure vessel welder's job. But Stan never really convinced her. "You could get him a job if you truly wanted to." she sniffed.

Dave King was more impressed with the way the plant fitted together, appreciating the complexity and yet essential unity of the process. He poured endlessly over the process flowsheet, trying to visualize the gas and water flows. The gas flow was really pretty simple. In a line between the towers and the road were the five compressors, one for each of the first stage towers, a slightly smaller one for the second stage, and a still smaller one for the third. Dave thought that the word 'compressor' was something of a misnomer as they did not do much compressing. Their real function was to circulate the H_2S gas through the towers. They did this with an enormous fan, about 8 feet in diameter for the big first stages, which was powered by an equally enormous electric motor. One of these motors might consume as much electricity in two or three minutes as a house would in a month. The gas was pumped into the bottom of the towers through huge, 4 foot diameter pipes, and exited at the top, where the pipe made a graceful U-curve to descend down the side of the tower and back into the suction side of the compressor.

Dave wanted to understand the real science. He'd read the simple descriptions of how the process worked, but that wasn't enough. How could they expect a guy to control a plant as complex as this, he thought, unless he really understands what's going on, what's important and what isn't? "Why do you need all that gas, and why H_2S anyway?" was his opening question.

Stan hesitated, marshalling his thoughts. Now he would have to sidetrack into deep physical chemistry, with exchange reactions, ionic mobilities and the like. But wait a minute. The deuterium atom is a fickle thing, and shares one characteristic with many people, the difficulty of forming permanent relationships. Perhaps that would provide a framework.

So Stan began, "The deuterium atom moves easily from one molecule to the next, so easily you can never be quite sure where it is. First, consider water, ordinary H_2O. If there is no deuterium, that is precisely what it is, H_2O. And if there is no hydrogen, you have pure heavy water, D_2O. But if there is a mixture, then things get more complicated. Much of the deuterium will be present as HDO, the 'half deuterated molecule'. Now, that's a nice little rhythmic phrase. You see, science can get quite poetic sometimes. Here, give me a scrap of paper." Stan scribbled out a terse little equation:

$$H_2O + D_2O \Leftrightarrow 2HDO$$

"That funny little split arrow combined with the equals sign means the reaction is reversible, so it can go either way. It is just another way of saying what has already been said, you never really know where the deuterium atom is. Now, not only is deuterium mobile in water, but also in gas. There is another reversible reaction when you mix water, containing deuterium, with hydrogen sulphide:

$$HDO + H_2S \Leftrightarrow H_2O + HDS$$

This shows the deuterium atom can move easily from the gas to the water, and vice - versa. When it's cold, the deuterium prefers to co-habit with a hydrogen and oxygen atom, so the deuterium is more likely to be in the water. And when it's hot, deuterium prefers to live with a hydrogen and sulphur atom, so, voila, you have it in the gas. That's the basis of our GS process. GS stands for 'Girdler-Sulphide', a process developed by the chemists of the Girdler Company, in the Manhattan nuclear bomb project of World War II".

"And are you telling me," said Dave, "that all we need to do is to keep one part of the mixture hot, and the other part cold, and we can get the deuterium separated from the water?"

"That's right," replied Stan. "Hence the technical name for the process, 'dual temperature isotopic exchange'. Now you can see why the process needs as much H_2S as H_2O. For every atom of water, there must be one atom of gas. Fortunately for the environment, it's only the water which is used and discarded; the gas remains in the process to be used over and over again. Rather boring for it, I should think."

The water flow was far more difficult to visualize than the gas flow, thought Dave. There were 57 heat exchangers arrayed in a neat line on the other side of the towers from the compressors, and a line of 20 pumps at the foot of the towers. The words 'dual temperature' was the Achilles heel of the GS process. All the water flowing through the plant had to be first heated to about 85 degrees Fahrenheit, for the 'cold' part of the process, then to about 265 degrees for the 'hot' part, and finally had to be cooled as much as economically possible before discharge to the Strait. Dave's mind began to boggle at the thought of running a single integrated plant with all this complexity. Sure, the refineries he had worked on were complex, but they were usually a set of distinct units with storage tanks, so that each unit could be started up, run, and shut down separately. In this plant, all of the almost 200 instruments and controls had to work properly for production to be maintained. All that rotating machinery, with its power systems, seal oil systems and bearings was going to be a real challenge, he realized. Since there was so much water, that took a lot of heat. Heat was energy, and energy cost money. Most of the heat exchangers were simply to save energy; the heat was piped from one part of the plant to another, as the needs of the process dictated. But, with the second law of thermodynamics being what it is, (briefly, you can't get something for nothing), a lot of heat was still needed, and that was where Nova

Scotia Power came in. Their plant was across the road, just to the south. The two plants were locked into a symbiotic relationship. They used oil-fired boilers to turn one million pounds per hour of water into steam at high pressure, generated some electricity from it, and then passed the steam in a large pipe to the heavy water plant at a much lower pressure of 150 psi. After most of the rest of the heat energy had been extracted by enormous heat exchangers in the GS process, it was passed it back to Nova Scotia power as condensed water. The two plants were using co-generation, long before the word became fashionable in an energy hungry world.

Stan was eager to see inside the towers under construction, since the heart of the extraction process, the sieve trays, were now being installed. Once H_2S gas was loaded into the process, it would be extremely difficult to enter, and he naively thought there might never be another opportunity. Oh, the innocence of youth and inexperience! So he, Dave, Gerry, and a few other newcomers, properly attired in gloves, duffel coats and hard hats, reported to the construction elevator at the base of C tower, the third of the three identical first stage towers. The elevator was a cage, about 6 feet by 4 feet, which rose inside a lattice work structure, 150 feet up the side of the tower. They crowded into it with the construction supervisor guide, and with a knee-jerking jolt, started a clattering ascent. Almost immediately, the cage cleared the clutter of piping and heat exchangers, and the familiar view of the Strait emerged. The cage, rattling up inside its lattice, seemed to have no obvious means of motion, but Stan caught a glimpse of the little gas fueled pony motor powering their ascent. Almost before he began to enjoy the ride, the cage stopped with a gut wrenching deceleration. The cage door opened, and the little band stepped out into a new world. Stan looked about in amazement.

The group was half way up the side of C tower, about 140 feet in the air, directly between it and its neighbor, B tower, which was about 20 feet away. Attached to both towers were scaffold platforms, on one of which the little party now stood. The two platforms were joined by a pair of twelve foot long planks, each about 12 inches wide, resting on the scaffold platforms at each end, and bridging the chasm between the towers. As a gesture to safety, a rope was strung loosely on one side of the planks, offering a rudimentary handrail. It was obvious that any attempt to use the handrail would be fraught with danger... it was so loose as to guarantee you would end up, like Tarzan, swinging by one hand over the gulf. Their guide, hands in pockets, strolled nonchalantly out on the planks, turned round and said, "They're just finishing tray 58 in B tower, and we can get in through the number 3 manhole. Follow me." The tyros were being introduced to the macho world of the steel erector, where indifference to, and even courting of, the dangers of heights was expected. Everyone followed him across. Like leaping out of the trenches in World War I, not to follow your mates would have instantly labelled you as less than a man. (Rumor had it that their boss, Don, had already frozen up in just such a situation.) Their guide was already walking round the scaffold platform to where the 18 inch manhole entry gaped into the tower. With a practiced gesture familiar to any submariner, he faced the tower, gripped the manhole edge, and swung himself, feet first, through the aperture. With more or less equal skill, and not a few grazed knuckles and scraped shins, the rest followed him in.

Now they were standing on another construction platform in the eerie half-light streaming in from the manhole. Below, the interior of the tower was lost in darkness. About thirty feet above, reached by a ladder, men were working in the glow of lights, installing the sieve trays on which the whole process depended. Each tray spanned the entire tower with a thin perforated stainless steel plate; there was a tray every 18 inches in this part of the tower. Alternating from side and center, a small vertical passage called a 'down comer' connected a tray to the one below. In use, gas would flow upwards, through the perforations in the plates, while water flowed across the tray from side to side, being rolled into a thick froth by the upwelling gas. The height of the froth was governed by the outlet weir, over which the water poured into the down comer on its way to the next sieve tray below. Thus was accomplished the intimate gas/liquid mixing on which the whole process depended.

Later, after describing how the process worked to a local reporter, Stan was amazed to read in the subsequent press article, that it worked 'by gravity.' "But you told me," the reporter answered in response to Stan's challenge, "that the water flows down from one tray to the next. If it wasn't for gravity, it wouldn't work." Stan had to admit the logic.

Still with the group inside the tower, but lost in his own thoughts of those capricious deuterium atoms making their choice between gas and water, Stan jumped out of his skin when a loud crash echoed through the cavernous chamber. A construction worker had dropped a large bolt to land deafeningly on a pile of plates beside the little group. Nervously, Stan tightened the strap of his hard hat. Only later did he realize that this was also part of the initiation ritual, the steel worker's way of welcoming the strangers to his world. The group made their way back to the ground, retracing their steps with the swagger of the neophyte.

The administration building had been finished early in construction. The new staff wandered through it like buyers surveying their new house, each mentally staking his claim to his own small piece of real estate. The building was about 60,000 square feet, and was built on a small rise to the north of the towers. A third of it, fronting south onto the process equipment, was two storied; the rest was of the same two storied height, but broken into two cavernous bays. The larger of these bays was the maintenance shop; the smaller was to hold the distillation unit for the final product, and miscellaneous smaller equipment. The control room, at the south-east end of the top floor, was an architectural masterpiece. Seventy-five feet long and twenty-five feet wide, the southern wall was unbroken windows with a spectacular panoramic view of the plant and the Canso Strait. Stan was lucky enough to get an office with a window on the same wall. Just opposite his office was the tiny space allocated for the laboratory. Downstairs were various rooms, many for the hourly paid staff. There was the so called 'surgery', where the plant nurse and part-time doctor would hold court, and a safety equipment room, where breathing equipment could be maintained and periodically recharged with fresh air. Both of these were located strategically close to the process area exit. The human relations manager also had an office downstairs to show his fellowship with the hourly paid employees, and strategically close to the main entrance to the building. Stan speculated privately whether that location was to allow him to be the first to greet visiting dignitaries, or to allow him first egress in the event of trouble.

In the large bay at the south-east end of the administration building stood the plant's 'piece de resistance', the DW finishing unit. DW was another hold-over acronym from the Manhattan project, and stood for Distillation, Water. The unit contained two gleaming stainless steel towers, about 60 feet high and 8 feet in diameter, which projected above the administration building. Being a slightly heavier molecule, heavy water boils at a temperature about three degrees Fahrenheit higher than ordinary water. So separation can be effected by continued repetitive boiling, in which the lighter $H2O$ vapor passes upward in a distillation tower, while the heavier $D20$ water falls downward. So, that reporter was right. Really, it only takes gravity to make heavy water!

An official from the Nova Scotia government presented himself to Stan one day. "I understand you are intending to operate a still on these premises," he said officiously. Stan paused and thought. He supposed they were soon going to operate what was undoubtedly a very large still. The only problem was it worked in reverse to the end result desired by the moonshiners, in that it concentrated the liquid with the higher boiling point, not the lower boiling point as in making alcohol. However, it sent the lower boiling point liquid back to the GS process, since even water only partially enriched with deuterium was too valuable to discard. The still could probably be adapted to provide moonshine in copious quantities, if fed with the right mash.

Stan kept these thoughts to himself as he replied, somewhat defensively, "It is actually a highly specialized heavy water distillation unit." The official ignored these objections. "Nonetheless, it is classified as a still, and accordingly must have an authorized licensee. Please fill out this form and sign at the bottom."

"Err, I suggest that I take you to see our plant manager", Stan argued.

"I have already seen him, and he has sent me to you, since this is a production matter." That is how Stan became the licensed operator of the largest still in Nova Scotia.

So far, the strangers from other countries and provinces had been spared the worst of Cape Breton weather. But as the summer of 1969 lengthened into fall, the characteristic gales began. Stan's first experience with them was quite minor. He had recently purchased a sixteen foot, wooden speedboat with a thirty-five horsepower outboard motor, which his family used for water skiing. He had tied it up in the angle of the fisherman's dock, protected from the waves and open sea, so that it could be seen from his bedroom window. One August night he awakened to howling wind and thrumming rain.

Looking out of the window, he could see nothing, but remained philosophical. "If it's gone, it's gone," he thought, "and I'm certainly not going out in this." Later he woke again. The rain had stopped, the wind seemed to have abated, and a fitful moon could be seen through scudding clouds. On an impulse, he put on a dressing gown, picked up a flashlight, and walked over to the dock. It was pleasantly warm, but the gale was far from over. Shining the light down onto the boat, he was appalled. The copious rain had almost sunk his boat! The stern was very low in the water, and the little wavelets in the lee of the dock seemed already to be lapping over the one or two inches of remaining freeboard. The bailer could be seen floating in eighteen inches of rainwater. Frantically, he left the flashlight on the dock and climbed down the ladder. The boat was so waterlogged it obviously would not bear his weight. With one hand, he groped for the bailer, holding onto a ladder rung with the other. A gust of wind wrapped most of the dressing gown round his head. Since he always slept 'au naturel', he was grateful that the moon chose that moment to chastely retire behind a cloud. The gust diminished, and the edge of the gown trailed in the water, only to flap about his thighs a moment later. Finally, he collected himself and began to bail. It had been a close call.

A little blow like that had no effect on the plant. But a few weeks later, shortly after noon, a real north-westerly began to howl down the Strait. Construction workers were sent home; nobody could work outside in these conditions. The first things to go were the plastic ducts housing the cooling tower fans. Watched from the control room, they contorted into strange shapes, and finally disintegrated, pieces of white plastic whirling away across the sodden landscape. Don, Len, and the construction supervisor came in from a tour of the plant and, looking grim, told Stan that the third stage towers were swaying in the wind. He couldn't believe it. Towers that were two hundred feet high and twelve feet in diameter were swaying? What kind of force could do that? Hurrying out to see for himself, it was hard to stand against the wind, and impossible to look into the rain. But making his way to the northwest end of the tower line, Stan found the shelter of a construction shed, and with his back to the wind, was able to look up and along the line of the towers. Swaying they certainly were. From the tower diameter, he could estimate they were moving about 12-15 feet each side of the center line, an amplitude of 25-30 feet. Curiously, they were moving exactly 'out of phase', that is as one moved to the right, the other moved to the left, completing a whole cycle in about a second, like the rhythm of two enormous inverted clock pendulums. A quick inspection of the base of the towers revealed the foundation was secure, so the towers were actually flexing, bending as a solid rod would do if held at one end and deflected at the other.

Returning to the office, Don and Len had already decided what to do. Stan was to learn how crucial it is not to be absent when important decisions are made. Don said, "Stan, drop everything, and get right on it. Find out what causes it and how it can be prevented."

Stan was thus thrown into the deep end of the discipline which came to be his favorite in North American management - problem solving. The less you knew about the problem initially, the better, as you were less likely to be biased as to the solution. You could count on someone, somewhere on this vast continent, being anxious to convince you they had the precise expertise you needed, and, for a price, stood ready to solve any problem you cared to present. In this case, it really was that simple. Stan found a wind tunnel in the Canadian Research Council in Ottawa. When Stan described the problem, the researcher hit on the cause and the solution, almost immediately. He pondered, "Hmmm… they were swaying exactly out of phase you say? Sounds like Von Karman vortices to me." So Stan asked him to explain.

"Well, when the air blows past a tall structure, vortices break away from the edge, alternately from each side. As they break away, there is a momentum transfer from the wind to the structure, which tends to set the structure swaying at its natural frequency. In your case, the towers are just about one diameter apart and the wind was coming at a slight angle, so the vortex which starts one tower moving to the right could just as easily start the second tower moving to the left."

"If that was the case, how could it be fixed?" asked Stan.

"The two towers could be braced together, which would raise the natural frequency, so that it would need the devil's own wind to excite them."

"How could that be proved?"

"For a paltry sum," in the researcher's estimate, not Stan's, "a model could be built, tested in the wind tunnel. This would show the towers swaying when unbraced and not when braced." The researcher indicated that he could also find out the critical wind speeds and directions for both braced and unbraced towers. And that is precisely what he did, and he was precisely right, and his solution worked out precisely as predicted. Len's engineers designed a bridge between the two towers which allowed each tower to thermally expand vertically on its own, but did not allow them to move sideways except in unison. The bridge was installed the following spring, and the towers were never seen to sway again, which was a pity in a way, because they looked very graceful and alive that day of the gale. Of course, as skeptics said, perhaps there was never exactly the right wind speed and direction again, either. But, Stan believed in the bridge and that wind tunnel project came out of his budget.

That particular gale also led to some strange events in town. Neighbors of Jane and Dave had put a small shed at the bottom of their garden. The neighbors were away as the wind began to tug at the home-built structure. With the shed swaying and rocking, the wind also began an insidious campaign on the foundations until finally the little edifice broke loose, and under the open mouthed gaze of the family, slid across the garden to come to a temporary stop against the side of the house. There it continued to sway and bang against the siding. Jane watched it for a few minutes and then decided on action. "Peter," she said to her young teenage son, "that shed is damaging the Brown's siding. And who knows where it's going next and what damage it might do. Look, there are some big garden stones in their yard. Nip out and put a couple in it to hold it down." Peter was thrilled to be allowed out in such weather.

The next day, before Jane could explain what had happened, Mrs. Brown was agog to tell her story. "Goodness gracious," she said, "what a storm. We had to pull off the road as Bill could scarcely keep the car on the road. And did you see what it did to our shed? Tore it off the foundations, blew it across the yard, and rolled a couple of our garden stones inside it!"

The plant was, to outward appearances, finished. All of the towers were complete, with their trays, and had passed the mandatory pressure test; all the pumps and compressors were in place; all the heat exchangers were piped into precisely the right place in the process; all of the hundreds of instruments and automatic valves were hooked back up to their respective controls and displays in the control room. The pace of construction was, almost palpably, slowing down. The construction gate was closed, the construction camp closed down, and now the remaining construction workers had to use the main gate like CGE employees. Most of the construction supervisors had returned to their USA or Ontario home base. Only insulation and certain small piping jobs remained to be completed.

The plant assumed the stately, impressive, impersonal air which it was to retain for the next 15 years. Coming into Port Hawkesbury from the north, say from St Peters or Isle Madame, the top two thirds of the plant rose majestically into view as you crested the last hill, dwarfing the plume of steam from the pulp mill. At night, the line of mercury lamps along the catwalks outlined the towers, and two ruby-red aircraft warning lights glowed from the top of the flare tower, creating the image of a giraffe or trumpeting elephant. It towered expectantly, almost defiantly. "Come on then, who is man enough to put me to work?" it seemed to say in silent challenge.

Now, consider the management team CGE had gathered to start up this highly dangerous, complex, 24 hours-per-day, 7 days-per-week chemical process. First, there was Don, tall, thin, autocratic, somewhat acerbic and, in Stan's mind, difficult to approach. He delegated completely, and rarely interfered with the work of his subordinates, unless asked. But watch out if he did. He would focus his sharp intellect on the problem presented to him, and you might not like his answer. He was a professional engineer, experienced in making nuclear fuel, which was, true enough, a job demanding high quality management. But, it was neither as risky, nor as challenging, as the job about to be embarked on.

Len was stocky, thorough, competent, always considering cost. He was an experienced professional engineering manager from CGE's lamp division, doing a tremendous job, but in a totally unfamiliar environment.

Phil Arrowsmith was a courteous, grave, somewhat formal, human relations manager, used to the relatively benign (some said 'sweetheart deals') of CGE/union relations. Now he was to be thrown to the wolves in the rough and tumble world of Cape Breton unions, with their coal miner heritage and distrust of management.

Bill Simms, the genial finance manager, was the one guy who seemed to be operating in familiar circumstances. Pennies seem to be pennies the world over, except Bill was dealing with an investment originally estimated at $50-60 million, but soon to exceed $100 million.

Rex Rich had recently taken over as Operations Manager, after the unexpected premature departure of his predecessor. Rex was a big, bluff, genial, man with on-the-job training at Quebec oil refineries. He was supremely self-confident, but with no professional qualifications, and not even suspecting of what he didn't know.

Stan was a nuclear physicist and nuclear safety specialist, with very little practical experience, and none related to chemical processes. He was soon to find out that he was in a job completely over his head.

It said something for the can-do spirit of Canada in the late 1960's that CGE even attempted the job that had to be done with the team then assembled. Nobody was goofing off, everybody pulled his weight, and nothing was omitted that was known to be needed. Could a more experienced management team have been assembled? Almost certainly. Could a more dedicated and harder working team have been found? Probably not.

Don was not worried by his neophyte management team. He had a couple of the best heavy water production consultants in the business at his beck and call. One of them, Dr. Victor Theyer, could be called, if not the father, at least the guardian, of the GS process, having worked for DuPont as they brought their pioneer version of the GS process into production in the 1950's. A slender, white-haired, diffident, yet erudite man, Vic relished his visits to Canada. He once said to Stan, "I always enjoy visiting Halifax on the weekend and driving over the harbor bridge. It isn't often you get to see almost half of a nation's navy at one time!" Vic was a lifelong

Republican, and used to lecture anybody who would listen on politics in the USA. "The unions have got it all wrong," he would say. "They keep asking for wage increases when they haven't increased productivity. Then we get inflation, and the government takes more of your money. What they should do is hold wages steady while productivity goes up. Then everybody can buy more with the same money, and the government takes proportionately less."

Don was no fool. He knew CGE was taking on a big job, but he had also visited a working heavy water plant on more than one occasion, and had listened carefully to what that staff and his consultants had told him. The messages were essentially two.

First, get your construction standards right. H_2S was a dangerous, poisonous, corrosive, gas. Yet, provided all the proper materials were chosen, and all welds were properly made and properly stress relieved, (a heat treatment after welding to remove any residual forces locked into the metal), it could be handled safely. So Don had retained RECO, the General Electric Real Estate Construction Organization, to manage the plant construction for him. They had brought up a number of skilled construction supervisors from Ontario and the USA. They were meticulous in keeping records of each weld, and the stress relief and X-ray which accompanied each one. Secondly, although the process was essentially simple to run, the best instrumentation in the world wasn't good enough. You had to be able to measure the concentrations of deuterium in the process, to high accuracy, routinely and rapidly, several times a day, and make process adjustments based on analyses of those measurements. Don had found that Atomic Energy of Canada, experts with heavy water, had developed new laboratory instrumentation capable of the necessary precision. He thought he had been lucky to find, in Stan, a physicist, who seemed unfazed by the technical jargon involved, and who would staff and run the necessary laboratory facilities.

Once the plant was up and running, Don had been told, there was only one other thing, which, while it would not prevent the process working, could limit the amount of product you could produce. That was a mysterious process called 'foaming'. It was poorly understood, since it had never been seen by anyone in water and H_2S mixtures, but seemed to be related to the purity of the water used. It occurred apparently on the top tray of the first stage towers, and had the effect of limiting production, since the only known remedy was to reduce the rate of water flow to the tower, and production was directly proportional to the amount of water passing through the tower. So Don had covered that base too. He instructed Len to design and build a miniaturized replica of the first stage tower, with a little gas compressor and water pump. They had brought this device to Cape Breton, filled it with local water and H_2S, and circulated the gas through the water. Much to Don's delight, there was no foaming, and the new sieve trays worked fine, at water flows even greater than those for which the plant was designed. So Don was sure that at the plant in Cape Breton, he would have no need for the complicated water treatment facilities which were a feature of the USA heavy water plant.

So, Don was fairly sure he had done everything any reasonable manager could do to ensure the success of this huge investment for CGE. As the plant neared completion, he racked his brains for anything they had forgotten. No, he concluded, all the bases were covered. Provided they were careful as they commissioned the equipment and started up the plant, nothing could go wrong.

3 GETTING READY

It was a peaceful Saturday morning in the spring of 1969, a beautiful day, still with a hint of winter in the clear air, and a growing sense of urgency at the plant. The engineering staff was increasingly busy as the various systems neared construction completion. A sixty hour work week was instituted, which was to last for almost three months.

Stan's laboratory had only recently become available, but at least Mark could get on with the business of training his technicians in tolerable, if still cramped, conditions. Until a few weeks earlier, he had enraged his laboratory technicians by setting up some equipment in a washroom, so they could start to learn simple water chemistry analysis.

On this particular day, Stan was goofing off on one of his favorite pastimes, touring the plant, with the unstated official objective of visiting every location in the plant where operators would draw samples for his technicians to analyze. His real objective was to climb the process towers to enjoy the spectacular view. The elevator, although working, was still under control of the construction crew, so he elected to climb the flare tower steps, looking for the flare tower sample points on the way up. At the 400 foot level, the steps ceased, and on an impulse, he climbed the remaining 50 foot caged ladder to the very top of the flare tower. Here there was a little platform surrounding the four foot diameter 'high pressure' flare stack. The smaller 'low pressure' flare stack also stuck through it. From here, Isle Madame, 15 miles to the east, was clearly visible. Stan even fancied he could make out his home in D'Escousse. The view from this spot was unmatched anywhere in Cape Breton - a 360 degree unobstructed panorama of the best of Cape Breton, the Nova Scotia mainland, St George's Bay, and the Atlantic. Still dizzy from the hyper-ventilation of the climb, he drank in the spectacle, until, sated and somewhat awed, he descended to the top catwalk.

There were three big service systems which the plant needed, electricity, water and steam. CGE was taking over the first system to be released by construction, the high voltage electrical distribution system. Leaning on the guard rail of the walkway, the substation was laid out 250 feet below in panoramic view. The building contained the high voltage distribution panels, and outside, the two 66,000 volt transformers. This tranquil scene was abruptly disturbed by a puff of smoke, curling out of the west door of the substation, followed by two electricians, running for their lives. The smoke thickened and steadied into a roiling cloud. Even from 250 feet in the air, Stan could hear a high pitched roar. There was an electrical fire, and it looked like it could be a bad one. He raced down the flare tower steps to join the growing throng around the substation. It soon became evident that there was a short circuit on the 'low' voltage bus of the No. 1 main transformer. 'Low' is, of course, a relative term. The transformer accepted 66,000 volts from the incoming Nova Scotia Power overhead distribution lines, and stepped it down to 6,600 volts for distribution within the plant. No one could mess with this 'low' voltage! There was no equipment for dealing with this kind of fire. The Port Hawkesbury fire department arrived, but stood by in impotence. Water, all they had, would of course be lethal. The smoke diminished, but the roaring continued, and soon a shout went up. "Here it comes!" was heard. The duct connecting the substation to the transformer began to glow cherry-red, then white hot, and finally melted in a blaze of sparks. This duct was about 18 inches in diameter, and contained the three 1 inch square aluminum conductors which fed power from the transformer to the substation. Now it became obvious what was happening. Somehow a short had occurred inside this duct, and an electrical arc had struck between the aluminum conductors. Since the power had not been disconnected, this arc continued to melt the aluminum bus bars, working its way back towards the transformer as it did so. If it could not be stopped soon, the transformer itself would catch fire. Normally, when this kind of short circuit occurs, an upstream circuit breaker would sense the abnormally high current, trip out, and disconnect the high voltage line from the power station. Why had this not happened?

Now, apparently help arrived from the Nova Scotia Power Plant, also under construction. An enormous pair of what looked like gas cylinders, on a two wheeled trolley, was dragged into the sub-station yard. It was a large 'dry chemical' extinguisher for electrical fires, intended to spray a powder on the electrical fire. Under heat, the powder would release carbon dioxide and so smother the fire. Willing hands seized the cumbersome device and dragged it into position. Completely impervious to the roaring crackling arcs only a few feet from him, Stan found himself at the sharp end, handling the hose nozzle. Marvelous luck! He would save the plant almost singlehanded, even though he had never used such a device before. "Turn it on!" he roared, pointing the nozzle at the fire, and striking a pose like a heroic fireman. There was a fumbling with the valves on the trolley... he was not alone in being new to its use. There was a little puff from the nozzle and then nothing. He stared in disbelief... this inanimate thing was preventing him from becoming a hero. More fiddling with the valves produced absolutely nothing. Disappointment, frustration, and rage coursed through him in successive waves. Only later did he find out the powder was caked solid from being left too long in a humid atmosphere.

Now everyone could only watch despairingly as the arc moved inexorably back into the transformer. Black smoke appeared again in copious quantities as the transformer oil caught fire. But finally the roaring stopped. Two Nova Scotia linemen appeared and announced they had manually disconnected the grid lines, four miles away at the Port Hastings substation. As soon as the power plant could ground the lines, the fire truck could extinguish the now harmless oil fire.

The obvious query was, "Why had no automatic circuit breaker operated to isolate the fault?"

The linesmen seemed surprised by the question. "Oh, there's new automatic fault protection due to be installed, but not for several weeks."

Don looked at Len. "We must call Reg." Reg Richardson was Don's boss, a vice-president of CGE. "I will need you to explain why we proceeded to commission the high voltage electrical system without adequate protection," Don said. Len's face was a study; he had been assured by the Nova Scotia Power Commission that the system protection was adequate, and he had been more surprised than anyone that the main breakers did not trip. However, he kept his counsel to himself in front of the crowd, and at least saved face for his boss.

The whole event had lasted about an hour. During this time, most of the power produced by the Nova Scotia power plant at Glace Bay, about 80 miles away, had been diverted into the wretched transformer. A colleague, who lived about half way between Glace Bay and Port Hawkesbury, reported that he heard his refrigerator 'running funny'. He measured the voltage in his home and found only 50 volts instead of the normal 110. That was because Glace Bay maintained the 66,000 volts at their end of the transmission line, while the faulty bus bar reduced it to almost zero at Port Tupper. He was half way in between.

The cause of the fire was never discovered. Something had intruded itself, accidentally or deliberately, inside the duct. Anything could have started it - a sandwich wrapping, a wet rag, a lunch pail, a mouse or a bird nest. Cape Breton was rife with unsubstantiated stories of what the locals would do to keep, or prolong, their jobs. At the adjoining oil refinery, a pipe fitter was reputed to have been caught welding a blank in an effluent line just before it was buried. The cause of the fire was never found, although Len favored the mice theory. Whatever the cause, the plant suffered for years to come. The actual delay to commissioning was quite short, since it was quite possible to run on only one of the two transformers. But it was impossible to properly clean the delicate protection circuit breakers in the substation after they were coated with soot, ash and oil. The electricians did their best, but inexplicable 'spurious trips', shutting off power to one bit of plant equipment or another, were to plague the plant for the rest of its life.

Chastened, plant workers resumed commissioning. Instrument air, which provided the motive power for many of the automatic valves on the plant, worked fine. The emergency diesel generator provided limited electrical power, not enough to keep the process running, but at least lit and powered the administration building and provided power to the elevator and to the fire pumps. This worked fine. And the non-interruptible power checked out OK. This provided electricity to all the instruments and controllers at the plant, without a break, even if the incoming power from the grid failed. All of these were essential safety systems.

After electricity, the second of our three major service systems was raw water. Surely nothing could go wrong with that. The water was pumped up from a forebay station at Landrie Lake, about a mile away, to a small head tank at the top of a little rise just outside our site fence. The delivery system seemed a mix of the modern and the old fashioned. The pumping station, although small, was neat and up to date. But the water flowed through a 48 inch diameter wood stave pipe, made just like a barrel, with iron reinforcing bars round it at regular intervals. It leaked like a sieve all its life, but never let the plant down. Shortly, Mark brought Stan the first water sample taken as it entered the plant filters. Stan looked at it dubiously. "That's not water, that's Cape Breton tea. What's it like after it's been filtered?"

Mark brought out a second bottle, of slightly weaker tea, which he had hidden in his pocket. Because most of the color was caused by very fine silt and dissolved organic material, neither of which was removed by filtration, the improvement was slight. The lake was newly bulldozed out of the characteristic red clay endemic to much of Nova Scotia. Felled trees were rotting on the banks, and every rain storm washed more silt and organic matter into the lake.

"Well," Stan said, with more confidence than he felt, "let it run a bit. Perhaps it will improve by the time we feed it to the process." But, of course, it didn't.

Stan voiced his concern over water quality to both Len and Don. "Look, we know water quality is important. At Savannah River, they have to reduce production on every slight upset in water quality. They reckon they get foaming, whatever that is. And their operating F factor is only 1.2, while our plant is designed for 1.6." The F factor was a measure of throughput, especially important in the first stage towers. The quantity of heavy water which the plant could hope to produce was directly proportional to the F factor.

His colleagues were reassuring. "Relax, Stan. We know all about that foaming business. That's why we ran the tests we did. And Cape Breton water, combined with these new Union Carbide sieve trays, is great. No problem. Go and read the report." Stan had already done this. He knew the pilot plant had worked fine up to an F factor above 1.6. Stan had no answer to this logic. He dismissed the problem. After all, he hadn't designed this plant. His job was just to run it the best way he knew how.

So the cooling tower bay was filled with the stuff. The cooling tower was a wooden slat structure, about quarter the size of a football field and 60 feet tall, which served several functions. The bay was a concrete basin several feet deep and covered the same area as the tower. It provided a reserve of water, for firefighting, and for short term loss of the raw water supply. The cooling water circulated through any of the process heat exchangers from which it was necessary to remove heat. The heated water was delivered to the top of the towers, and allowed to run down over the slats. Gravity was at work again. Big fans at the top of the tower, enclosed in plastic ducts, could increase the air flow, and thus provide extra cooling. By this means, the water in the cooling tower bay could be kept at precisely the right temperature, summer and winter. And finally, the filtered incoming water was mixed with just the right amount of this warm water to provide the 85 degree Fahrenheit feedwater which the GS process required.

Finally came the time to start the symbiotic relationship with our neighbors, Nova Scotia Power, and get the third of the major service systems going - steam. The power plant pressured up the big steam delivery main which ran under the road between them and us. For days, the plant echoed to the roar of sundry vent and drain valves as operators purged the various lines. Each first stage tower was provided with a pair of vertical heat exchangers designed to accept steam. Either one of the pair could be cooled by either that part of the process which needed heat, or by cooling water from our cooling tower. With any three of these exchangers working, the entire 1.05 million pounds per hour of 150 psi steam, which Nova Scotia power was contractually obligated to supply, could be accepted. On warm summer days, when the air was dry, a rare event in Cape Breton, you could hardly distinguish that the cooling tower was operating. But most days, and especially in the winter, an enormous cloud of steam would billow out from the fan ducts. One of Stan's most memorable sights was the plant in winter, with snow all around, a clear blue sky framing the gigantic towers, and five columns of steam rising from the cooling tower fans to dissipate in the clear, cold air. Beauty is in the eye of the beholder, they say.

Stan's laboratory had started up a very advanced instrument, developed by Atomic Energy of Canada, for measuring deuterium in water at low concentrations. Mark had reason to be proud of his technicians, but of course, with European understatement, he didn't show it. Here they were, really just kids out of school, routinely using a sophisticated mass spectrometer, which only a few months before was a research tool in one of the most advanced nuclear research laboratories in the world. Gerard was soon to become an expert on this instrument, and could dismantle it down to the last nut and bolt, clean it, and restore it to pristine condition.

However, not all the laboratory equipment was working as successfully. There was a problem with the gas chromatograph, which seemed to be almost beyond both Mark and Leo's capabilities. This instrument, fairly new in the world's chemistry laboratories, would measure the proportions of H_2S, nitrogen, and other trace gasses, in the process. It would be needed soon, so Stan began to look around for a consultant to start it up. Hiring an expert full-time would be counterproductive, since the measurements would rapidly become routine, and too boring for a career PhD. The Czechoslovakian engineer, Otto, heard of the problem and advised Stan to talk to his wife.

Stan knew there were company policies governing the hiring of relatives, and so he accosted the human relations manager. "Phil," he said breezily, "is there anything in CGE policies which would prevent me from hiring the wife of an engineer?" This was 1969, remember, and the words 'sexual discrimination' were almost unheard of. Phil was the master of the 'pregnant pauses' technique. When you are not sure what to say, say nothing. Perhaps the other guy will divulge something useful. But Stan was now used to that ploy, and sat quietly waiting.

"Why would you want to do that?" Phil eventually asked.

Stan explained his problem with the gas chromatograph. "Here we are, 1000 miles from anybody who might be expected to know anything about such an instrument, and it turns out that Otto's wife, Helen, who is in Port Hawkesbury, did her PhD in gas chromatography in Prague. If I can't use her, it's going to cost the company a mint to bring someone in from Ontario or the USA."

Phil looked uncomfortable; the mention of a dollar cost had clearly established Stan on the offensive.

"It is not the policy of the company to hire close relatives into what might become a supervisory relationship," Phil replied somewhat stiffly. "It could be prejudicial to discipline."

"But Otto's in engineering and Helen would be in the lab." Stan objected.

"You can never tell." Phil replied, "If Peter left and Otto was promoted, and then an organization shuffle put the lab in engineering, Otto might find himself trying to discipline his own wife, or even recommending salary increases for her." After further discussion, they finally agreed that since Stan's need was relatively short term, he could offer Helen a consulting contract, not employment, for a period of up to 12 months. So Stan called her in for what was to be one of his stranger employment interviews.

Helen was an attractive woman, and like her husband, was in her late twenties or early thirties. She explained that she and her husband had worked for a national research organization in Czechoslovakia. She had graduated in chemistry and then got a PhD, working on the theory and calibration of gas chromatographs. They had both escaped from Czechoslovakia in the late 1950's when the county took its brief fling with democracy, which was soon suppressed by the USSR. Granted asylum in Canada, they had lived in Toronto and learned remarkably good English. Otto had seized on the job which Len offered. Like Stan, they didn't care if Cape Breton was at the ends of the earth. It was a good, permanent job with prospects. They had two small girls. Stan could hardly stop from rubbing his hands with glee. Perfect. She would probably not want a full time job with the two children, and as a consultant, she could choose her own hours. Stan explained that he would want her to start up and calibrate a gas chromatograph for just a few simple gasses, then train junior technicians in its routine use. The whole project should only take a few months, and he was prepared to offer her a consulting contract for as long as the job took.

As he spoke, to his surprise, her face darkened. Finally Helen could no longer contain her fury. "That is what is wrong with the capitalist system," she burst out. "You use people as long as you need, and cast them aside when you have no further use for them." Stan was thunderstruck. Here he was, trying to do a co-worker's wife a good turn, and she wanted to preach socialism at him. His first impulse was to chuck her out, but perhaps something could be saved from this disastrous interview. He managed to get her to calm down, and as they talked further, they drifted into generalities. Later in the conversation Helen mused, "Of course, we could not have children in Prague."

"You mean you knew you might escape, and did not want the burden?" he asked.

"Oh, no, it was a condition of employment," she said. "If I became pregnant, I would have lost my job."

Stan could hardly believe his ears. Now he had her. "That is what is wrong with the Communist system," he raved in mock rage. "It interferes in peoples private lives. I could never impose that as a condition of employment in this country." She grinned and they parted friends. But, she never came to work for Stan, and finally Leo found a specialist from CGE in Ontario who helped him get the gas chromatograph up and running.

Standing in front of the control room windows, Dave thought he had never seen a finer control room in his life. The view of the plant process area was superb, and that of the Strait of Canso nothing short of spectacular. Turning around, the instrument and alarm panels faced him in a panoramic sweep. There was one panel for each tower, one for the water treatment area, one for the DW unit, one for the purge and stripper, and a separate panel for the electrical distribution controls. His panel operator, Bob, was working with Dave, one of the electrical engineers, and a team in the field, to 'ring out' the various control and alarm loops, meaning that they were checking them for function and continuity. There were hundreds instruments and controllers at the plant, and a special mnemonic had been devised for their identification. 'RC' stood for (rotating) compressor, 'RP' for a pump, 'X' for a heat exchanger, 'AV' for an automatic valve, 'I' for an instrument, etc. In addition, each part of the process was allocated a series of numbers, 100 - 300 for the first stage towers, 400 for the second stage tower, 500 for the third stage tower, 600 for the purge and stripper, and so on. His operators talked to each other in a strange sort of argot, reminiscent, thought Dave, of the chat between astronauts and their ground control, which was just pervading the national consciousness as the moon landing approached. A radio call from the field, "AV-361 is not stroking fully," instantly told the expert that the automatic flow control valve, controlling the level of water in the third of the first stage hot towers, was not moving through its full control range. "Close AM-610," radioed from the control room to an operator in the field, was a request to close the feedwater isolation valve to the purge tower. "IM-956 loop is open circuit," made clear that the high pressure flare header pressure transmitter was not reading in the control room.

The alarm panels were especially impressive. Running the length of the control room, occupying a space about four feet high between the panel and the ceiling, they contained hundreds of alarms in two inch by four inch translucent plastic-fronted boxes. Their purpose was to alert the operator to a process variable, such as flow, pressure or temperature, which was out of normal operating range. Each was color coded. Blue was a 'first level' alarm, normally meaning it might show at start up but would soon extinguish. Amber meant action should be taken, and red normally meant automatic protection had already operated, and that a piece of equipment had been automatically shut down. Since the operator's desk faced out overlooking the process area, he normally had his back to the alarms, which were equipped with a pleasant sounding audible 'pong' when they first lit, to attract his attention. During these days of 'ringing out', the control room was a noisy place.

To start up such a complex process, for the first time, with a highly toxic gas such as H_2S, would clearly be very dangerous, and would not give the operators a chance to get familiar with running their equipment. Instead, the plant was to run initially with nitrogen. Although there would be differences, chief among them the fact that nitrogen is much less soluble in water than H_2S, and of course the fact that no heavy water could be produced, the delay was considered justifiable for its safety, training, and 'shakedown' aspects. Now, the plant reached a fervor of activity as preparations for actually running the GS process went on apace. Pump and compressor motors were 'bumped', that is, briefly switched on and off to verify electrical connections and direction of rotation. Pipe lines were flushed to get rid of the debris of construction, rags, old lunch bags, etc. The nitrogen was brought in by huge rail cars and charged into the towers to a pressure of about 200 psi. Piping and towers were pressure tested to ensure their leak tightness. And then water was fed to the process. Rather to everyone's surprise, the whole process seemed to run very smoothly. Someone remarked, "Well, after all, it is only pumping water and gas around. If we can't do that, we need our heads examined." That remark was to come back to haunt everyone.

Time and luck was about to run out again. Commissioning had overtaken the construction crews, who were racing the weather to finish the heat tracing and insulation.

There is one aspect of the GS system which renders it totally unsuited for a cold climate. When H_2S and H_2O are mixed under pressure, a strange solid ice-like compound, called a hydrate, can form. Its chemical formula is $H_2O \cdot 6H_2S$, meaning one molecule of water joins with six molecules of hydrogen sulfide to form a solid. Just one problem: this ice forms at 85 degrees Fahrenheit under the pressure of the GS process. Stan suspected this is where Kurt Vonnegut got his idea for ice-nine in his Si-Fi novel *Cat's Cradle*, in which a scientist invents a form of water which freezes at 85 degrees Fahrenheit. There are a number of hydrates with similar properties. (In Vonnegut's novel, this strange form of water is eventually accidentally released, and turns all the water on earth solid.) Anyway, what it meant was that any water in the GS process will freeze if its temperature drops below 85. Not so good in the Canadian climate.

So every water-bearing pipe had to be steam traced and insulated. Steam tracing was just small diameter stainless steel tubing, typically somewhere between 1/4 and 3/4 inch diameter, which was strapped to the pipe to be traced. Steam was fed in at one end of the tube and condensed water, condensate, taken out at the other. With the size of the plant, there were literally miles of steam tracing tubes, and hundreds of individual steam tracing piping loops. Finishing the steam tracing had taken much longer than expected and the insulation of the piping, which could only be done after the tracing, was lagging, if you'll excuse the pun. Here it was mid-December, and much of the process piping was still bare. Bare piping didn't matter as long as the process was running.

But on this chilly December evening, with Dave on the night shift, disaster struck. The power plant suffered a total loss of their capability to make steam. This had happened before, and, with no control over the temperatures in the process, Dave ordered the inevitable shut down. The muted roar of the big compressors and pumps died, and an eerie quiet settled over the site. Initially, Dave was not concerned. Usually the Nova Scotia Power operators were able to restore one of their two main boilers fairly quickly, and if not, they had a 120,000 lbs./hr. auxiliary boiler which could at least keep the steam tracing supplied. As the minutes ticked away, the steam header pressure remained stuck on zero. Dave made increasingly desperate calls with no avail; apparently they had a strange electrical distribution system fault which immobilized their entire site. He notified Len, who sent engineers over to the power commission to assist, still with no result. There was no H_2S in the system, so Dave was not worried about hydrate as the process temperatures fell below 85 Fahrenheit. But as the evening wore on, a stiff north-westerly wind started to blow out of a clear starlit sky, and the air temperature began a steady decline. Dave was not worried about the big lines. An 18 inch diameter pipe filled with hot water would take an awfully long time to freeze. But the heat tracing and smaller pipes were a different matter. He consulted with Len and his engineers, knowing there was not much time left if the temperature continued to decline as precipitously as it was now doing.

So he gave the order to manually open all the steam traps, and drain the condensate accumulated in the steam tracing tubing. A steam trap is a little automatic valve at the end of each heat trace tube which opens under the steam pressure to discharge accumulated condensate, and closes when there is no more water in the tube. But, then another problem developed. The steam tracing piping had been 'field run', meaning the precise locations of each tube and steam trap were left to the tradesmen doing the job. There were no drawings, and each trap had to be located by eye. In many cases, a collection of traps was to be found in midair, 20, 40 or 60 feet above the ground. When installed, scaffolding was present, which had now been removed. Frantic calls for ladders began to come in, which immediately depleted the supply in maintenance stores. The job was just too big, and even though engineers and supervisors joined the crew in the field, not much could be done. To Dave's fevered imagination, the silence of the plant became the quiet of the grave. When he left at midnight, steam was still not available. It was, in fact, not restored until the early morning hours.

Next morning, the plant presented a sorry sight. Under a clear blue sky, it was wreathed in steam from hundreds of leaks. Many steam trace tubes had been split by ice, and, after steam was restored, condensate had dripped over piping, pumps and motors. Long icicles were everywhere. Worse, some of the steam tracing tubes and traps had not thawed, and the steam tracing was inoperable. The temperature remained below freezing for weeks, and many defective lines were not found until a thaw set in. Large kerosene fired heaters, called Giant Salamanders, were tried which could blow hot air into areas of the plant draped in canvas tarpaulins, but it was not very successful. Somebody was heard to say that less hot air was needed, not more. Much already installed insulation had to be removed, either to repair split trace tubes, or because it was so damaged by water as to be useless. The delay prolonged start-up into the summer of 1970.

With time, all the problems of the winter were resolved. The electrical and steam systems were working, fairly reliably, and even the water quality had improved slightly. The plant was once again running smoothly with nitrogen instead of H_2S, and the insulation and steam tracing damage had been largely repaired. By now, everything to prepare for production had been done, with one exception. The mainstay of the process, poisonous H_2S, had yet to be faced.

4 PARDON ME...FIRST GAS

As for most people, Stan's first introduction to hydrogen sulphide, or H_2S, began at school. He could still remember filching a small quantity of calcium carbamide from the chemistry laboratory, and adding water to it in an inkwell. The mixture began to bubble satisfactorily, while the horrible aroma of rotten eggs pervaded the toilet in which he was working. To put the vile concoction in the locker of a friend, he had to conceal it under his school cap and walk the corridor. His cap stank abominably for several hours afterwards. But now schoolboy pranks were behind him. The plant would require more than an inkwell of the gas to operate properly. More precisely, it would require about 600 tons. And as he had learned only recently, H_2S could be lethal in minute quantities.

The Atomic Energy Control Board, which was responsible for the health and safety of the Canadian public in matters pertaining to nuclear energy, had asked CGE for a safety report and hazard analysis for the plant being built at Point Tupper. Stan had recently been hired from England specifically for expertise in nuclear safety, so Don obviously, though mistakenly, thought he was a natural for the job. Nuclear safety analysis is usually concerned with the release of radioactivity into the environment and the consequent risk of cancer sometime in the future. He soon realized this was unlike any nuclear hazard analysis he had ever seen. H_2S can be lethal, not at some time in the future, but now, right now. It might be detectable in air, at about one tenth of a part per million, by its characteristic 'rotten eggs' smell. But by the time it reaches about one part per million, it paralyses the sense of smell. People gassed and subsequently resuscitated typically report only a faint, sickly, sweetish odor. At somewhere between five hundred and one thousand parts per million, it paralyses breathing. No fuss, no pain, no gasping for air, just a simple collapse. If somebody doesn't get a breathing mask on you, under pressure, and force oxygen into your lungs within a few minutes, you are 'a goner'. The only good news is that H_2S is bio-degradable into harmless water and sulphur, so if your breathing is restored, there are no harmful side effects. H_2S is a particular hazard in fishing boats, when cleaning out rotting holds, and in the oil industry, when cleaning sour oil tanks, and even in sewers. Several people a year are typically killed by trace amounts of this gas while working in these industries.

Fortunately, the Du Pont Company, who was running a smaller version of the same heavy water production process in Savannah River, Georgia, had learned how to handle the hazard with the minimum of risk. There were three basic principles: First, everybody who entered the gas process area wore a small breathing air bottle with the face mask clipped to their shoulder harness. The mask was always in the 'demand' mode, delivering pure air when the first breath is drawn, so that at the first suspicion of gas you could clap it on your face and get out of the area pronto. Second, everybody who entered the gas process area worked with a 'buddy', a companion who watched out for your well-being. If you were gassed, your buddy's responsibility was to protect himself, raise the alarm, and render aid, IN THAT ORDER. Third, everybody was provided with little rolls of lead acetate tape, which turned black at the slightest exposure to H_2S. All of these measures, and more, were implemented. A series of red gas alarm buttons were placed at strategic locations around the plant, with special attention to the higher and less accessible places, such as the tower catwalks hundreds of feet in the air. These buttons rang an alarm in the control room on a special panel, so that the operator could see instantly in what part of the plant a gas release or gassing had been reported. They activated a special ear-splitting audible alarm, which was rapidly named the 'Jesus Christ' alarm, because those were usually the first words said by the shift supervisor whenever it was activated. Rescue packs, large twin cylinders of breathing air, with full face masks and auxiliary masks for resuscitating victims, were also placed strategically around the plant. And finally, there were the gas detector alarms, situated around the perimeter of the plant, supposedly capable of detecting H_2S at the 1 part per million levels.

The plant safety supervisor, Tom Campbell, led the training activities. He was a bluff, down-to-earth guy from a New Brunswick oil refinery. He started drills for the operators where they had to rescue supposed victims from various, not always easily accessible, locations. He needled management to invest in the best possible fire truck that money could buy. If he had been able to find one with a ladder capable of reaching the tops of the towers, he would have bought it! He acquired a dummy on which both resuscitation and heart massage could be practiced. The laboratory made up small sample bottles of water with dissolved H_2S, so the smell could be experienced, and the effect of the gas on the lead acetate tape could be seen firsthand. By and large, the operators were receptive to the safety precautions; they realized it could mean the difference between life and death. The same could not always be said for others at the plant. As the time of first gas on site approached, full safety procedures were put into effect, and drills without advance warning were initiated, even though no gas was yet on site.

The first such drill was not an unqualified success. Dave and Ken had to visit the process area. Dave was a Polish Canadian, second generation, with an unpronounceable name, and an inclination to be serious. Ken was from British Columbia, and took a somewhat lighter view of life. Both were electrical engineers, Dave specializing in instrumentation and Ken more into the high voltage stuff. Both had taken the safety training, which was mandatory if you needed to work in the gas process area; both had qualified as buddies. It was a fine, dry, spring day, and a delicate aura of anticipation was spreading through the plant as the time for the first H_2S shipment was drawing near. They donned their breathing equipment, checked their lead acetate paper, put their personnel tags into the buddy control rack, and walked out into the process area. Dave had already been briefed by his boss, unbeknownst to Ken. Near the base of the third stage tower, Dave gracefully slumped to the ground in a fair imitation of a gassing victim. Ken looked down on him, completely forgot his responsibilities to his buddy, stirred him with the toe of his boot, and said, "Come on, Dave, quit mucking around!"

To be fair to the engineering staff, they also adopted the safety procedures wholeheartedly once gas actually came on site. The same could not be said for some of the maintenance technicians, who sometimes appeared to view these cumbersome practices as a form of management harassment. Perhaps this was symptomatic of the worsening labor relations to follow. For example, certain maintenance procedures which required breaking into a pipe containing H_2S called for a safety monitor. His function was solely to watch the job being performed, and ensure all the safety practices were being followed. This gave the union a problem. Paying someone to just watch was rather novel in Cape Breton, and was obviously to be encouraged. But there was also the undertone of constant supervision by a poor chap who could be called to task by management if his buddies took a short cut. The union gave grudging acceptance to this, and other, safety practices.

Safety of CGE people on site was one thing, but what about the neighboring industries and communities? When analyzing the so-called 'offsite' hazard, Stan had taken into account the weather patterns, and the largest release of gas considered to be 'credible'.

Credible was a wonderfully imprecise word, much in vogue at the time, in all sorts of safety reports. He surmised the largest credible gas release would be that occurring from the instantaneous and complete rupture of a 2 inch diameter H_2S bearing pipe at 280 psi pressure. The analysis showed that if this accident happened, at ground level, under the worst weather conditions, fatal gas concentrations could be expected up to over a mile away.

Credible, of course, means different things to different people. CGE was very concerned that the plant be safe, and there were numerous reviews with a variety of 'experts' to ensure that nothing had been overlooked. But at that time, there were few experts in chemical plant safety, despite the fact that many chemical plants are more risky than the nuclear plants which were, and continue to be, the subject of so much misguided concern. Bophal, the chemical plant disaster in India, had not yet happened. In the USA at the time, much effort in nuclear safety was being devoted to the so-called 'worst credible accident', an imprecise oxymoron if ever there was one.

At one of the several safety reviews, while Stan was making a presentation to numerous management and safety reviewers, a USA engineer threw him a curveball. "I understand your contention that a 2 inch diameter pipe failure is the worst credible accident," he said, "but the towers have 24 inch diameter manholes. What happens if one of these blows off?"

Stan could not believe his ears. He thought, "Who was this guy, and what was going through his mind?" Stan did some rapid mental calculations. Let's see, the area of one of those manholes would be about 2000 square inches, so each pound of gas pressure would exert about one ton of thrust. With 280 pounds per square inch of gas pressure, that means the reaction force on the tower would be 280 tons! If that occurred at the top manhole, over 200 feet above the ground, the overturning force on the tower would be immense.

"In that case, sir," he replied, "the tower would probably fall over". Stan did not add that since the manholes were on the opposite side of the towers from the administration building, the tower would probably fall right on top of the control room!

Anyway, the answer seemed to satisfy the questioner. He nodded gravely, and the review proceeded. The question and answer contributed precisely nothing. The manholes were bolted to the tower with eighteen 2 inch diameter bolts... it was inconceivable thst one could blow off. But everyone has his own way of getting comfortable with novel situations, and being an old hand at the safety business, Stan knew there was nothing like replying to a curveball with a curveball.

The adjoining industries also had to be considered. Gulf Oil, adjacent to our south-east fence, was really no problem. Their management was familiar with H_2S hazards, and their people were trained accordingly. That was fortunate, because they would be downwind for much of the year. The Nova Scotia power plant, which provided us with both electricity and steam, was across the road that lay along our south-western border. The Strait of Canso, running roughly northwest to southeast, imposed its own microclimate, and winds from the northeast were quite rare. So the risk to the power plant was small. But the pulp mill, about half a mile to the northwest, seemed worried. They used a sulphite process, in the course of which H_2S was generated, but not stored in large quantities as we intended to do. They had limited experience with H_2S and apparently, did not like it. So it came to pass that CGE was invited to a meeting. The invite came through Phil, the human relations manager. Courteous, formal, and somewhat grave in his business dealings, Phil was the epitome of a large company HR manager. He was always aware that when he spoke, people would naturally assume that CGE was speaking. Therefore, he said as little as possible. Those in the know, of course, would automatically discount anything the HR manager said as irrelevant or, more likely, soon to be reversed by head office. Needless to say, he did not have an easy time of it with the blunt Cape Bretoners. As a defense mechanism, Phil had perfected the 'pregnant pause' technique into an art form. When you thought you had said all there was to say, and it was his turn, he would say nothing and give a slightly encouraging nod of his head. On more than one occasion, Stan had found himself pouring out his heart, when all he really wanted to know was the CGE policy on, for example, moving expenses.

Phil had no idea what the pulp mill wanted to discuss, as on this particular morning, they walked into a pulp mill conference room. Present were a mixed bag of management and union personnel, and the atmosphere was downright frosty. In the center of the table was a large tape recorder. The opening words from the mill management were accusatory, very much in the form of 'have you stopped beating your wife yet?' In essence, the management said that since CGE was about to introduce this very significant risk into what had previously been a peaceful industrial community, what we were going to do to protect their workers?

Then the tape recorder was switched on, and one of Phil's pregnant pauses developed. Stan opened his mouth to speak, closed it again, and looked to Phil for guidance. Phil finally spoke. "If you'll turn that damned thing off," he said, "perhaps we can talk."

Stan was amazed and delighted. Never had he been as proud of a CGE manager as he was at that instant. They went on to have quite a constructive discussion, which culminated in open communications between the two control rooms. Subsequently, it was rumored that current pulp mill union/management relations were not good. Some operators had been chased down a passageway by a mixture of noxious gasses, and the union was, probably quite reasonably, demanding more breathing equipment. Management was balking, and somebody dreamt up the bright idea of having CGE supply it! Stan was never able to verify this story, but it certainly explained one of those otherwise inexplicable Cape Breton happenings. Through Phil's adroit handling of a potentially difficult situation, conflict had been turned into co-operation.

Finally, there was the question of the safety of the residential communities around the plant. The only significant population was Port Hawkesbury, about 1-2 miles to the northwest, with Port Hastings about a mile further, perhaps 2000 people in all. Mulgrave, right across the strait, was nearer, but less populous, and the wind almost never blew that way. Most of the plant staff that lived in the town were not really worried. They felt that the likelihood of an accidental release of gas large enough to be a hazard to the town was so remote as to be completely discounted. But that view was not shared by everyone.

In particular, the Atomic Energy Control Board, as part of its license to allow plant operation, had required CGE to develop an emergency response plan for neighboring communities. Stan had not the faintest idea how to start. In actual fact, he started with the Emergency Measures Organization in Halifax. This was a small federal government coordinating agency, principally focused, at that time, on alerting the population in the event of a nuclear war with Russia - an event Stan considered much more likely than a large gas release from the heavy water plant. This organization convened a meeting with 'interested' parties, most of whom were decidedly disinterested. The Royal Canadian Mounted Police, now mounted in Chevrolets, were the only people who maintained a twenty-four hour capability in the area. They would have at least one car, perhaps more, in the area of roughly 30 miles around Port Hawkesbury. It was not obvious what could be done with this grand resource.

At this meeting, Stan committed one of his better 'faux pas'. Being not long out of England, he was not familiar with the entire Canadian vernacular, and made the following remark, "Well, we have very few people on the night shift, and we certainly can't spare a shift supervisor to go round and knock up the sleeping housewives."

There was one of Phil's pregnant pauses, and then general laughter. In vain, Stan tried to explain that the profession of 'knocker-up' was very important in early industrial England, when few people had alarm clocks, and to be late for work could easily cost you your job.

The meeting finally settled on a list only of things which could reasonably be done. CGE undertook to provide an on-site siren, which would be sounded in the event of a 'large' gas release, and a wind direction indicator, so that the shift supervisor would know where the gas was drifting. Community education, through practice drills, and press and radio announcements, would encourage people to stay indoors if this alarm sounded. A standard emergency announcement with the local radio station would be established. A flashing light sign at two locations on the road past the plant would be installed to warn people not to proceed if a gas release was in progress. Finally, the shift supervisors would be provided with a sports rifle and incendiary bullets. The objective of this would be to ignite any large release of H_2S which did not ignite spontaneously - the gas would burn to sulphur dioxide, and the heat of the flame would disperse the gas more widely.

Of all these precautions, only the road signs really served any purpose, and even here, on the few occasions when they were used as a precaution, people would often drive blithely past, assuming it must be some sort of drill. The siren raised an almost painful banshee wail on site, but could hardly be heard in the town, certainly not indoors, particularly if you were asleep. Neither the radio messages, nor the incendiary bullets, were ever used, although practice with the rifle was always the shift supervisor's favorite drill. And so, the plant was as ready as could be for the big day of H_2S delivery.

The H_2S storage area consisted of two large spheres, each capable of holding 400 tons of gas, as well as miscellaneous pumps, compressors and heat exchangers. A small concrete block house contained a little local control room. The complex was located in the western corner of the plant, where a railroad spur line allowed rail cars to be brought into the plant. Unfortunately, the H_2S storage unit was also only about 100 feet from the public road to the west of the plant, on which hundreds of construction workers daily drove to work at the Gulf Oil refinery site, oblivious to the danger.

The H_2S gas was shipped from Alberta, as a liquid, in insulated and pressurized tank cars. It was arranged that the first gas delivery would be in the smallest tank car available, 40 tons, to allow the plant staff to cut their teeth with the smallest risk possible. One morning, there sat the first delivery. To the uninformed, it was just another rail tanker, probably carrying oil or something equally commonplace. Stan was fascinated by the innocuous, but somehow mysteriously malevolent, small black tanker. His overactive imagination visualized it rolling through Toronto, through sleeping communities, past schools and hospitals. What would happen if there was a train crash or a derailment? What confusion, what panic, what publicity! Only a decade later did a derailment of a toxic gas (not H_2S) rail car in a Toronto suburb give rise to all Stan had foreseen. His son and daughter-in-law were evacuated in that derailment, along with hundreds of thousands of others.

With the arrival of the first tank car on site, Gerry felt that the plant was really beginning to 'cook', and he was relieved to see that the effort on the safety systems was redoubled. All of the standing fire hydrants were flushed and checked. They were equipped with monitors, fire nozzles on swivels, which could be turned to spray water almost anywhere in the process area. The plant perimeter was equipped with six sets of H_2S monitors, each sniffing the atmosphere for the deadly gas. The H_2S monitors were complicated devices, which needed constant tender loving care to function properly. Moreover, they would frequently respond to the sulphur dioxide, continuously released in trace amounts by the neighboring pulp mill. When the wind swung unexpectedly in the right direction, a shift supervisor might nearly experience a heart attack, as the H_2S area monitor signaled the presence of gas in the air. Finally, they learned to relate the alarms to the wind direction and the pulp mill effluent, logging the events accordingly.

Most of the staff took safety training seriously, but a few, even some of Gerry's peers, treated the safety training with cordial derision. "They should know better," Gerry thought. This plant was immense and awesome. It was not threatening, perhaps, if you understood and respected it, but certainly not to be trifled with. One day, he felt, they would need all their safety training, skill, and courage to control the monster sleeping within. So, he redoubled the safety training on his shift.

The tank car was unloaded by connecting it to the storage area with a high pressure flexible hose, about one inch in diameter. H_2S

can cause a special problem in steel, called hydrogen embrittlement. What happens is the hydrogen dissociates from the sulphur, and passes into the metal. Hydrogen is funny that way, being one of the few gasses which can quite readily diffuse through solid metal. When it does so, otherwise quite ductile metals can become very brittle. Now for a hose, which by its nature has to be capable of bending, you want the steel to be ductile, otherwise it may crack. Fortunately, at the low temperatures used, the reaction was quite slow, and the hose steel was heat-treated to keep it ductile. Several rail cars had been unloaded, over the course of a few weeks, before the inevitable happened.

Fortunately, Gerry was the shift supervisor that night. Gerry was one of the few operators who came from Alberta with extensive 'sour' gas experience. 'Sour' is the term for natural gas contaminated by H_2S. Indeed, the reason the plant's H_2S came from Alberta is that the natural gas in that province is contaminated by H_2S, which must be removed before distribution to consumers. It was no accident that Gerry's shift had participated in unloading each of the previous tank cars. When his shift came on duty that night, the unloading hose had already been connected from the valve at the top of the tank car to the valve on the piping of the unloading station. The latter had a motorized valve, to isolate it from the H_2S storage spheres, which could be operated remotely. But the valve on top of the tank car could only be opened or closed by hand. Gerry prowled the area suspiciously. You couldn't be too careful at times like these. He watched his operators conduct a pressure test, using nitrogen gas, on the hose and its connections to the tank car. Containing 80 tons of gas, it was twice as big as the one they had first unloaded. He watched his senior operator climb the ladder of the tank car, and, 15 feet in the air, crack, and then fully open the valve to the hose. In the little control room, he watched the last motorized valve open, and the pump start. Now liquid H_2S was flowing from the tank car into the storage sphere. Gerry relaxed. Everything was working fine. He made sure his operators knew what to watch for and what to do when the tank car emptied, and began the walk back up the hill. Perhaps he worried too much, he thought. He had barely reached the administration building when the piercing notes of the 'Jesus Christ' alarm filled the air. His radio crackled to life. "Gerry, the H_2S storage area alarm has rung in", his control room operator warned. The familiar lurch in his stomach seemed to focus his brain. He wrestled on one of the big breathing sets stored just inside the door, turned, and ran back towards the H_2S storage area. Even from here, he could see a white mist pouring from the tank car loading station. Inside the H_2S block house, his operators had already shut down the pump, closed the automatic isolation valves, and were struggling into their own forty minute breathing packs.

"Come on," Gerry said grimly, "Masks on and let's go see what we've got." Unfortunately, it was an absolutely windless cool, autumn night, a rare event in Port Hawkesbury. As they approached the tank car, a writhing, white, miasmic mist was pouring from the top of the car, spilling down its sides, and spreading towards them. The H_2S was actually an invisible gas, what was visible was the water vapor condensed out of the air as the gas cooled on expansion through the leak. Gerry's co-workers regarded it with horror; through the visor of their masks he could see their terrified expressions. Walking around the loading platform for a better view, his worst fears were confirmed. The hose was leaking! Unless that manual valve on top of the tank car could be closed, the entire 80 tons of H_2S would be released. While bad enough, the incident was not as bad as it seemed at first glance. The rate at which the liquid H_2S was escaping was really quite slow, and if any sort of wind had been blowing, the event would have been easily handled. Gerry knew what had to be done, and he knew instinctively he had to do it himself. His compatriots were too scared, too out of their depth, too unsure of themselves, to behave rationally in these circumstances. He drew their attention as he flipped his breathing regulator to positive pressure breathing, and watched as they did the same. Now no gas could enter the masks, since the pressure inside was always higher than that outside. But now there was no time to waste; a forty minute pack would last barely twenty minutes on positive pressure breathing. Steeling himself, he walked through the evil cloud, scaled the ladder, and closed the valve.

Later, Stan tried to understand what was going through Gerry's mind when he made that heroic, altruistic, decision. "Well," Gerry said, "two things were pretty obvious. First, the valve had to be closed. We couldn't just sit there and let it leak for days. And second, my other operators were scared as hell. You see, they didn't yet have confidence in their breathing equipment."

"But weren't you scared?" Stan asked. Gerry looked at him in surprise.

"You helped select that equipment," Gerry said, "and you know when you turn to positive pressure breathing, instead of demand breathing, you're going to get just pure air, right? What was there to be scared about?"

The event caused considerable soul searching on Stan's part. "Could he have done it? Would he have had the courage to wade through that gas in the interests of other people?" Musing, he tried to place the essential difference between Gerry and himself. "Trouble is," he thought, "I'm always asking, but what if this or that bit of equipment fails? Gerry had absolute reliance on that breathing equipment". He thought further, "There seem to be two kinds of bravery. There's recklessness, when you don't know, or don't care, about the risk you take, when you're fired up by adrenalin, or by the suffering of a companion, or by the exhortations of your pals, or when you just act instinctively. Then there's Gerry's kind, where you know exactly what the risks are, believe that they can be managed, or at least controlled, and do what has to be done. I think the second kind is superior to the first." Stan did not want to admit that he did not possess either.

5 IT REALLY WORKS

Stan could never remember how he came to be elected as the management representative to remain on site when the first H_2S was to be transferred from storage to the GS Process. "Something like the swaying third stage towers," he thought, "not being present when the crucial decision was taken. Or perhaps he volunteered, or was maneuvered into volunteering." Anyway, on this warm summer night, with all other management having pressing personnel business elsewhere, he reported back to work after dinner to see how the evening shift was progressing.

Gerard, the shift supervisor, was cheerful but evasive. "They're going through the checkout procedure now, shouldn't be long. You know we have to check out all the H_2S monitors round the site?" Stan did know. His lab had prepared little bottles of H_2S saturated water, which when waved under a sensor, would produce the desired alarm. With maddening slowness, the checkout proceeded. About 10 pm Gerard came to see him with what looked like relief on his face.

"The monitor in the H_2S storage area isn't working, and the instrument technician on site can't fix it. I guess we'll have to wait till tomorrow." Now Stan's natural stubbornness came to the fore, aided by a desire to just get on with it and an inward determination not to be beaten by fate. Also, he didn't want to have to explain the delay to Len and Don tomorrow.

"Heck, no," Stan replied. "Miles said he checked them all out today. Let's call him in." Miles Gardiner was an instrument engineer from the USA, who had pulled off that almost unknown feat, a transfer from GE to CGE. He once told Stan he didn't agree with his taxes going to the Vietnam War, and since he was in his fifties and a bit old for civil disobedience, had done the next best thing. He lived out near St Peters, about thirty miles from the plant, and had adjusted instantly to the Cape Breton way of life. His wife was a teacher at a local school, which, combined with his working at CGE, caused the locals some confusion.

"She's got a good job there?" was the spoken question often addressed to him, followed by the unspoken thought, "Then why are you working?"

Miles admitted he did not have a good answer. He appeared about midnight, complaining Stan had gotten him out of bed, and wanting to know why it couldn't wait till tomorrow.

"It is tomorrow." Stan said, and personally buddied with him down to the suspect instrument. Meanwhile, the graveyard shift had come on duty. The new shift supervisor, Jim, did not have the same concerns as Gerard. Jim had worked in the Athabasca tar sands project, and had an Albertan oil and gas worker's familiarity with H_2S. Grumbling, Miles and the shift instrument technician pulled the instrument apart and put it back together again.

"That seems to be working now." Miles muttered.

"What did you find wrong?" Stan wanted to know.

Now it was Miles's turn to be evasive, "I can't be sure. These are tricky things."

Stan doubted that there had been anything wrong with it in the first place. And so, about two o'clock on a fine summer night, the first H_2S was introduced into the process. It was transferred very cautiously, so cautiously the flow was too small to read properly on the flowmeter in the transfer line. The only way to check how much was added was by the level change in the H_2S storage sphere. Stan stopped when he estimated the requisite ten tons had gone because Len and Don had instructed him, the previous day, to be conservative with the first charge of gas. There was no change in any of the process variables; it hummed along like a well-tuned machine.

"Get a gas sample from one of the first stage towers," Stan requested of Jim, "and leave it for the day shift to analyze. There are about 400 tons of nitrogen in there, so if we added ten tons, it will show about 2.5% H_2S. I'm going home to get some sleep."

The next morning Stan showed up about midday, expecting the accolades of his peers. Don and Len were polite but skeptical. "If any gas was transferred last night, why can't the lab see it?" they wanted to know. Leo and Stan conferred over the gas chromatograph trace. The big nitrogen peak was obvious, but where H_2S should be was the tiniest of tiny blips.

"If that's H_2S," said Leo, "It's not more than a few tens of parts per million."

Doug came up with the probable solution. "Look, we know H_2S will combine with iron to form iron sulphide, FeS. There's probably, oh, a million or more square feet of iron in that process. How much H_2S would that take?"

Some quick order of magnitude calculations showed that even if the iron sulphide layer was only a thousand of an inch thick, it could easily take a few tons of H_2S, and more, to coat all the surfaces. There was nothing wrong with what that valiant little band had done last night. It just had to be done again, and again and again. And over the next few weeks it was, still in small amounts, until all shifts became comfortable with the procedure. When the H_2S reached a few percent in the process, and safety training and safety equipment readiness were judged to be acceptable, Len and Don went for broke. On a Thursday, instructions were left to transfer 50 tons per night for the next four nights. That would replace most of the nitrogen, which would be eliminated automatically by the purge and stripper unit, and leave about 200 psi of H_2S in the GS unit. Then the process of lining up the unit for production could begin the following week.

So Stan went home that weekend feeling pretty good. The H_2S was building up, the process was running smooth, the summer was here and it was time to get some water skiing in. So he was surprised to get a call from the plant on Sunday morning. "Good morning, Mr. Davies. Mark here."

As if he didn't know. Who else would call him Mr. Davies, and in that accent? "Hi, Mark, what's up?" Stan asked.

"Congratulations, Mr. Davies. You've done it."

"Congratulations? I've done what?"

"The process, Mr. Davies. It's working."

"Working, but how? It can only be about 80% H_2S and we haven't lined it up yet."

"None the less, Mr. Davies, there is already 1000 parts per million in the third stage."

"That's great! I'm on my way in."

There was one peculiarity of the GS process which Vic Theyer had emphasized to Stan time and time again. The ratio of the liquid flowing down the towers to the gas flowing up had to be precisely right. It was called L/G, and if L/G wasn't precisely at 0.52, the process could not work at maximum efficiency. In fact, the precision needed was about 0.1%, and since no flow meter could approach the needed accuracy, it was necessary to sample the process frequently, and to make small flow adjustments, to be sure it was set up correctly. Stan had assumed this would be a difficult and time consuming process, needing several trial and error iterations. But he had overlooked that since Vic was, of course, absolutely right for maximum production. The process would work at some lower level even if the gas and liquid flows only approximated the correct value. Doug had instructed the shift supervisor to set the flows approximately right, assuming the flow meters were accurate. Then Mark, bless him, on his own initiative, had gone in on that Sunday morning and persuaded the shift supervisor to draw a set of samples. Stan suspected Mark wanted to run his lab techs through the routine he had drilled into them once more, to make sure there was no hitch on Monday. To their surprise, Mark had found some enrichment in all the towers, although not to the design values yet.

So the plant was up and running, off to the races. Congratulations flowed in from all quarters. Reg, Don's boss, who had really been instrumental in persuading the CGE board and parent company GE to make the necessary investment, was in seventh heaven, of course. But, he also threw Stan a curveball, by asking when they would have first reactor grade product. That, of course, was the only thing CGE could sell and begin to recoup the investment. The question caught Stan flat-footed. "Let me talk it over with the guys, Reg, and I'll be back to you," Stan promised.

The 'talk over with the guys' was not encouraging. Doug estimated that the total inventory of heavy water in the entire process, when all the design concentrations were reached, would be about 50 tons. At the design rate, 100 lbs/hr, that would only take about six weeks to reach. But at the low pressure at which the plant was currently running, production was only half the design rate, so it could take twice as long. The plant was temporarily out of H_2S and, even though more was on order, the pressure could not be raised for another several weeks.

However, Doug came to the rescue by pointing out, "Look, it's not that bad. We can start feeding product to the DW long before the deuterium concentration reaches 45%. (It's design value.) The

DW won't work at its full rate, but it should produce something, even if we feed it with 10% product."

So Stan went back to Don and Reg cautiously optimistic, estimating reactor grade product about two months from now, say late October. He didn't add, "Assuming everything keeps running." That was a proviso he was soon to use to qualify every production estimate. Experience is a bitter and cruel teacher.

The first intimation of trouble ahead came, as usual, from Mark. Routine samples of water fed to the process were taken every shift, as were samples of water leaving the process and running to the sea. The former was really a precautionary routine; there was no known reason for any rapid changes, and the principal interest was the turbidity, which was a measure of the clarity of the water which we were feeding to the process. The effluent ditch was routinely sampled for H_2S, really a CYA record keeping measurement, to show anybody who might need to know how clean a process we ran. (CYA, for the un-initiated, means 'Cover Your Ass'). Mark brought in a sample bottle of water and put it on Stan's desk. "What do you think of that, Mr. Davies?" It was crystal clear, beautiful looking, drinking quality water.

"Pretty good, Mark. Where did it come from?" Without immediately answering, he put another bottle beside it. This Stan immediately recognized from its cloudy appearance as feedwater.

"Mr. Davies, the second bottle is what we are feeding into the process. The first bottle is from the ditch, what we are taking out. Where is all that mud going?"

At first, Stan's mind refused to grasp his question. Then Mark's full import became clear. The feedwater typically ran at a turbidity of about 10. That was roughly equivalent to 10 parts per million of solids. Even at the present 50% production rate, about 40,000 lbs./min water were going into the process. That meant about 500 lbs./day of solids were being carried into the process. And from the look of that ditch sample, precious few were of them were coming out. Stan conferred with Leo and Doug. They all agreed that Mark was probably correct, considerable solids were being deposited in the process. But where? They had no idea.

Leo put forward the most optimistic view. "Look, those first stage towers are huge. If it's just settling out at the bottom of those towers, which after all is where the water is almost stagnant, or at least moving very slowly, we could put tons and tons of the stuff there and it would not affect the process one iota."

Doug was not so sure, "Well, it's early days yet. I think the operators are beginning to feed more steam to those heaters. Perhaps they're fouling."

Once more Stan brought the matter of water quality to Don and Len's attention. But there was nothing they, or he, could do. To shut down only a few weeks away from first production, on the flimsy evidence available, was unthinkable. Don was reassuring,"Let's get into production first. Then, if the lake water doesn't clear up, perhaps we can look at some water treatment options next year."

Consistent with Doug's predictions, the concentration of product in the third stage rose steadily by about 0.5% per day. Those idyllic days of August 1970 passed in a rosy glow. The process really did operate as steadily as a rock. The samples rolled in, the lab did its thing, and everything seemed clear sailing, except for the inevitable communications problems of the various nationalities.

In Stan's operation, there was, of course, considerable interest in the analysis of the GS water samples for deuterium. The practice was to make only one flow adjustment a day. Samples were drawn about 10-11 am, 6 pm, and 2 am, and the resulting laboratory analysis would usually be available about 2-3 hours later. A flow adjustment, if deemed necessary, was typically made at the end of the day shift, about 3-4 pm. This particular lunchtime, Doug, Leo and Peter Chau were sitting in their office, eating the Kentucky Fried Chicken which they, and some of the guys in the lab, had ordered. Peter was a young Chinese engineer, still perfecting his English. He rummaged around in the various boxes, grumbling, and finally phoned Mark in the lab. "Hey, Mark. Have you guys got 'de salt?" Mark was very sensitive, some said secretive, about his technician's analyses, and refused to disclose any results until he had personally signed off on all of them. Accordingly, he was constantly chivied about the delay, and had been known to physically eject engineers hanging around in his lab.

"No. We have no results", Mark growled stiffly in his Polish accent.

Peter was not deterred. "Well, what about some ketchup?"

Now Mark got really incensed. Would these young process engineers never learn how difficult it was to get quick, reliable, analyses out of partly trained Cape Breton youngsters? "No, we have not caught up" he roared. "I will tell you when the results are ready."

Peter was now really mystified. "I thought you said you had no salt. What are you mad about?"

"We have no results" screamed Mark, and banged the phone down. Such were the challenges of a multi-national workforce.

While things were truly going well at the plant, there was one minor hitch. After about two weeks, the deuterium concentration in the third stage stopped increasing, and stuck at about 5%. Instant confusion resulted, or at least instant after the twenty four hours it took to show up on the chart and to be confirmed by the lab. Doug was mystified. "I don't understand it. The first stages seem to be producing as normal, but the third stage inventory isn't increasing. Perhaps we've got a leak." The shift supervisors were sure there was no leak, insisting it would be detected by the H_2S, but Stan had them search for it anyway. He also called Vic, who was equally mystified, and promised to come in.

On the morning Vic was due to arrive, a red-faced and embarrassed Mark presented himself in Stan's office. He almost groveled, "Oh Mr. Davies, how can you ever forgive me. The lab, my lab, has made a terrible mistake. I've let you down, I've let everybody down."

Stan had a moment's wild thought, "You mean we really haven't made anything at all?", but quickly suppressed it. "Come on, Mark, it can't be as bad as all that. What's happened?"

With much self-abasement, the story finally emerged. Mark knew that, at above a few percent of deuterium, he was supposed to switch from the mass spectrometer analysis to another technique, based on refractive index. But he had spent so much time drilling his technicians in the use of the mass spectrometer that he had not really familiarized himself thoroughly with the new technique, let alone trained his staff. He had run a calibration on the mass spectrometer up to about 4% deuterium, and it seemed to be nicely linear. So he had let his technicians go on using the mass spectrometer, above the range for which it was calibrated, while he prepared and calibrated the refractive index method for routine use. It was really a pretty simple technique, and Mark had assured Stan it was ready to go. But with his typical thoroughness, he couldn't put it into routine service until he had personally checked it out once more. Once he did so, the awful truth emerged. The mass spectrometer was incorrect for these high deuterium concentrations, and the last few days analyses had to be discarded. Stan listened with growing impatience. "Come on, Mark, don't keep me in suspense," he finally bellowed, "What the hell is the damn third stage concentration?"

Mark hung his head. "It's 7.5%, Mr. Davies. My lab has made a serious error. And to think we've bought Dr. Thayer all that way up from the USA for nothing." Stan could have kissed him, which with Mark's homely countenance, was a real measure of his relief. There was nothing wrong with the process, and production was on track

But Mother Nature sets her traps well for the overconfident. The first intimation of the shape of things to come arrived about the last weekend in August. Joy and Stan had friends over for Sunday dinner, and were just sitting down to the evening meal, when the phone rang.

It was the guard from the plant. "Mr. Davies, there has been plant shutdown, and H_2S is being released. The emergency call-in has been initiated." The emergency call-in was a standard list of key people whom the shift supervisor could request the guard to call if he felt the situation was getting out of hand, and he needed help.

Stan made his apologies to their guests, and took off like a rocket for the plant, his mind awhirl. "Gas being released! My God, where was it coming from?" he thought. His Dodge Challenger, a nice sports sedan, screamed round the bends of the winding Cape Breton roads. Just outside Port Hawkesbury, there was one stretch of about a half mile straight uphill. He had always promised himself, one day, to let her go at this point. At the bottom of the hill, he floored the accelerator, and rocketed over the top, still accelerating, at about 95 mph.

At the plant, the emergency, if an emergency it ever was, was already over. The NS power plant had lost all steam, so the heavy water plant had shut down. A few minutes later, they were ready to go back on line. To accommodate them, and to protect against dangerously low temperatures, one of the big first stage steam heaters had first to be transferred from process (meaning H_2S laden water) to ordinary cooling tower water. This was routine, but had always been done before with nitrogen in the process. This time one of the big isolation valves had not closed completely and H_2S laden water had leaked into the cooling tower, producing the familiar odor over a wide region. Gerard, the shift supervisor, had quite correctly initiated the call in on the smell of H_2S, even before he found the problem.

The operators were able to fix the problem by taking a few more pulls on the valve's big hand wheel. Actually, the mishap had apparently helped in another way. Algae had begun to grow on the slats of the cooling tower; it was to be recurring problem, especially in the summer. The dose of H_2S had killed it all.

Now Dave's shift was to be the first to restart with H_2S in the process. Problems appeared almost immediately. For example, when a first stage compressor stopped, all the water which was held up on the trays as froth, drained into the bottom of the tower and some overflowed into the big gas pipe leading into the tower from the compressor. This water, H_2S and all, had to be drained before the compressor could be started. But no provision had been made to rid of its H_2S, so it went right down the drain and into the effluent line. As a result, the effluent ditch stank to high heaven and the H_2S in air monitor over the ditch rang in. There was little Dave could do. He ordered more raw water to be released to the ditch, to dilute the gas to the maximum extent possible, and grimly hung on as the foul odor permeated the site and the surrounding area. "My God," he thought, "is every start-up going to be like this?"

Dave had done enough start-ups with nitrogen to know that the most risky part was yet to come. He ticked off in his mind the key checks in the start-up procedure, which he called out for his operators to follow. "Let's see, we've got a degassing tower running to the flushing drain, and the lab's verified the water is oxygen free. We've verified AV361 strokes, and we've got a level reading in the hot tower. There's steam going to XS601, and the strippers are ready to go. XS321 is drained and ready to accept steam. RC601 is online and circulating, and the purge and stripper pressures and tower levels are OK. John is draining the compressor suction line now. Is there anything I've forgotten?" He fidgeted and fussed as his operators in the field worked through their last check lists.

Finally, to his relief, John called in, "OK, Dave, that suction line's empty. I can see gas slugs in the sight glass."

"Right." acknowledged Dave. "You and Rory go to the compressor, and stand by to adjust the seal oil system. I'll send Ron and Jim to the purge and stripper." With all his team in place, Dave hesitated once more. "Hey, Bob," he said to his panel operator, "call the power commission and tell them to expect a few bumps in the power and steam demand." Then he pushed the compressor start button. The lights dimmed briefly as the 7000 horse power motor took up the load. Bob started a purge tower bottoms pump, and Dave cracked open AV321, starting water flowing. Inside the tower, water began to flow across the top tray, but with gas flowing upward through the sieve tray holes, water could not flow down to the next tray. Eventually a 5 inch froth accumulated, water began to spill over the downcomer to the next tray, and the process repeated itself. Now there was nothing to do for almost half an hour, and again Dave fidgeted and fussed as he waited for the next key indication.

"Here comes the cold tower level." reported Bob, as water flowing down the tower reached the midpoint, and a cold tower bottom collector tray level began to read. He started RP301 and lined up the dehumidifier loop for cooling.

"Okay, John, that compressor should be OK for a while," Dave instructed his first operator field team. "Get up by XS321. We should be putting steam to it in about 20 minutes. I'm always worried about water hammer in that condensate line."

Now, Dave knew, the critical few minutes were fast approaching. Cold water was making its way down the tower, tray by tray, about one tray every 30 seconds. Soon, the hot tower bottoms level would begin to increase and water would have to be released to the stripper to prevent the tower flooding. But now, unlike in his previous start-ups, the water would be saturated with H_2S. He had to get that water hot, real hot, before he released it to the stripper. He watched as Bob, seeing the hot tower level begin to rise, started RP311 and fed steam to XS321. Now the humidifier loop was operating, heating the water in the bottom of the tower. He alerted his operators standing by in the purge and stripper area, and positioned himself by the critical control panel. "OK", called Bob. "I've got about 350 degrees on IE326. Ready?"

"Let 'er come," replied Dave shortly. Bob cracked open AV361, letting H_2S saturated water flow from the tower to the much lower pressure flash drum. The effect was rather like taking the cap off a car radiator while it's hot, or shaking up a can of beer, and opening it. The gas bubbled out of the liquid as froth, what the specialist calls a 'two phase mixture', meaning there is liquid and gas present at the same time. Down in the process area, AV361, a specially designed 'letdown' valve could now be heard doing its work, crackling and banging away. Even though it was twenty feet in the air, it sounded like ten thousand pans of bacon frying.

Now came the time when Dave cursed the designers, "Why had they made this stripper so small? To save a few bucks," he supposed. He wished the guy who made that decision was here now. He'd give him a piece of his mind. As the automatic level control valve on the flash drum began to open, the level in the stripper began to increase. Dave poured the steam to the stripper reboiler and anxiously watched the stripper bottom's temperature. If he couldn't get it hot enough before the stripper level reached 100%, he'd have to shut everything down. And all his guys' efforts would be wasted, and he'd have to apologize to Gerry when he came on at midnight. Also, they would have wasted another eight hours potential production time. But Bob had done a good job. The water reaching him was nice and hot, and IT601 was already 365 degrees. He cracked open AV602, and the now H_2S - free water streamed out to the ditch, on its way back to Mother Nature, "We really only borrow it for an hour or so," Dave thought to himself. He watched as Bob and the field crew completed 'lining up' the process. First, Bob set the tower feedwater and gas flows on automatic at the same values used before shutdown. Then he set the hot tower letdown valve on automatic, followed by the flash drum and stripper level control valves. Down in the field, his operators confirmed RC601 was operating OK. This compressor took the gas released from the tower hot water, re-compressed it to about 200 psi, and fed it to the purge tower. Here it met the incoming water, and since cold water can hold much more gas than hot water, the gas dissolved and was carried back with the water into the tower. As Bob sat down at his data logger desk and began to punch in numbers, checking the temperatures at various points in the process, Dave began to relax. The first H_2S restart had gone OK.

With similar efforts from another shift, a second of the three first stage towers were soon restarted. One of the towers remained shut down to fix a compressor problem. When the second and third stages came online, another difficulty of running a plant of this size came to light. It took days to get the plant lined up and producing properly. The problem was that the inventory of deuterium got all mixed up at shutdown. There was already over ten tons of it in the process, based on three weeks of steady production at about 50 pounds per hour. Now the process must be lined up, that is get all the liquid to gas flow ratios set correctly, with that inventory in place. If the operators and Stan's engineers weren't careful, it was even possible to send some of the precious inventory back out to the strait, which was to happen on more than one occasion in the years to come. Even when properly done, a four to six day delay after a plant shutdown was not unusual, before the process was again in full production. Stan was worried as he had promised reactor grade product by the end of October. The plant was now down to only about 33% extraction, at low pressure with one first stage shut down, and had lost a week to boot. The third stage concentration resumed its upward trend, but at an even slower rate.

Even so, in November of 1970, the climax of the long haul, the culmination of all the efforts and the resolution of all the problems, was at hand, or so was the conventional wisdom. The product stripper, which removed H_2S from the third stage output, was put into operation. Water containing about 10% deuterium, and free of H_2S, began to flow, 'up the hill', and into the DW area of the administration building. Here it went into one of two weigh tanks, 10,000 gallon stainless steel tanks mounted on scales. This 'intermediate product', as it was called, was already so valuable that every drop would be sampled and weighed for mass balance purposes. The mass balance assured that all the deuterium was accounted for, and there was no leakage or loss. Now the DW unit was started, with intermediate product as its feedstock. Rather anticlimactically, a few days later, sampling indicated the DW product was ready. The DW operator steam cleaned one of the 45 gallon stainless steel drums provided by Atomic Energy of Canada, and filled it with the DW product. This sampling was not to be entrusted to any Tom, Dick, or Harry. Mark, with much fuss and care, drew the drum sample and retired to his laboratory. He emerged a half hour later to pronounce it acceptable. The plant had produced its first saleable product!

In contravention of all the laws of Canada, a small 100 ml sealed bottle of clear heavy water sits on Stan's desk shelf, along with other memorabilia of his career. It is labelled 'Reactor Grade D_2O 99.775% (by wt.)' in his secretary's neat typing. Reactor grade heavy water is a proscribed substance in Canada, and probably in the USA also, because it is a possible route to the production of Atomic Weapons. But fear not, it will never fall into terrorist hands. To Stan, it remains one of his most cherished possessions. After all these years, it remains unclouded and pure, almost pristine, with no indication of the superhuman efforts expended on its behalf in those tense fall days of 1970.

While all these earth-shaking events were happening, the compressor of the remaining first stage tower had been repaired and the tower was started up, connected to the other towers and aligned for production. Several more rail tank cars of H_2S had been unloaded into storage. Now everybody was truly ready to take 'their baby' up to full production. Everything worked; it remained only to show the world what CGE could really do.

Late on a misty afternoon in early November, Rex, Dave, and Stan gathered around for the ritual of writing the day book orders. The day book was where the operations manager put his intentions for the plant for the next 24 hours, or on weekends, 72 hours. It would contain instructions, for example, on equipment to be prepared for next day's maintenance, any special samples or process changes, instructions on any shipments of raw chemicals expected, and so on. Rex left instructions to raise the pressure SLOWLY, to its design value of 280psi, over the next twenty four hours, and to increase the feedwater flow commensurately. The next morning, all was on track. The pressure was coming up slowly, and all seemed at peace with the world. It was to be the last peaceful day for many months. By the next day, H_2S charging complete, the process was clearly in trouble. The second and third stages were running fine, but the first stage level control was very erratic, and as a result the water delivered to the stripper fluctuated severely, in both temperature and quantity. The familiar stench of H_2S filled the air from a 'sour' effluent ditch as the operators struggled, often unsuccessfully, to keep the stripper functioning properly. There was really very little instrumentation for such a large process, and it was not possible to tell what part of the tower was not working. But the classic Savanah River 'foaming' problem was suspected, for which there were only two known solutions. The first was the use of an 'antifoam', a silicone based chemical which suppressed the formation of bubbles, and the second was to cut the water and gas flow until the tower steadied down.

Antifoam was tried first, with zero effect. The trouble was that the antifoam was known from the Savanah River experience to have limited usefulness. It only worked over a very limited range, and obviously that range was not where the plant was currently running. So water and gas flows were reduced, progressively and in sympathy, to maintain the all-important 'L/G' ratio. The next problem was soon evident: the big 48 inch 'butterfly' valves in the suction of the first stage compressors were soon closed as far as they would go. These valves were provided with minimum flow stops, a mechanical device to prevent further closing. Frantically, Stan asked the chief engineer if the flow could be cut more. Peter said cautiously, "The minimum flow stop is to prevent stalling the compressor. But I think it can be adjusted to give you a bit more control."

That leeway was soon used up. Now, the compressors were screaming like banshees, protesting the miserably small flow of H_2S which was reaching their whirling blades. Samples showed the first stage towers were far off their optimum production settings. Before plans could be made to reduce the gas pressure, which was the only other way of reducing the gas flow, a crisis intervened.

That cool November evening, just before Stan left for home, the piercing notes of the 'Jesus Christ' alarm filled the air. He hurried into the control room, and met Gerry coming out, his face grim. "There's a gas leak on the suction pipe of B tower, and it's caught fire. It could be bad. I'm going down to take a look." They buckled on escape packs, and hurried down the steps and out into the process area. B tower was the middle of the three first stage towers, and the suction pipe to the compressor was the enormous 54 inch diameter loop which prevented water from a shutdown tower finding its way into the compressor. A leak in that could be very serious indeed; Stan gave silent thanks that it had caught fire. As they reached the compressor area, they could see a jet of flame, the characteristic pale blue of H_2S, jetting out sideways about 5 to 10 feet, from a flange on the suction pipe. The operators already had fire water monitors spraying adjacent piping to keep it cool. Following standard safety procedures, there was no attempt to extinguish the flame. A burning H_2S leak was normally less dangerous than one which could not be seen. Serious though it was, Stan mentally breathed a sigh of relief. At least the pipe had not failed at a weld, which was his perennial fear. And the leak was between the two gigantic gas isolation valves which isolated the compressor for maintenance. Once those were closed, and the compressor vented to the flare, the gas leak would be trivial.

Gerry was talking on his hand held radio to the control room, and came over to Stan, his face even grimmer than before, "They can't get the suction side gas valve closed. We might have to vent the tower." For some reason, perhaps if the fire had damaged the control cables, the big gas valve was not responding to the control room command to close. There were about 100 tons of H_2S in B tower which would surely leak out through that same flange, if something was not done quickly. Gerry gave orders to hook the fire pump into a drain valve on the compressor; he would flood the compressor and pipe with water if necessary, which would at least reduce the gas leak. But it also had the risk of putting out the fire and damaging the compressor, both most undesirable consequences. The flame burned with a dull roar, but, if anything, its length seemed to be increasing. Stan knew that H_2S was extremely corrosive, and wondered just what was happening at that damaged flange. Perhaps the gasket was even now being charred and corroded, preparatory to blowing out. Gerry was talking with his number one GS area operator and his buddy. Finally Gerry nodded, and they left. "They've volunteered to close that valve by hand," Gerry reported.

Stan was aghast. "But that valve is only a few feet away from the flame. It must be hot as hell up there and reeking with SO_2. And if the flame goes out, they're thirty feet in the air, on that little platform, right in the H_2S!" he protested.

"They know all that. They'll have their 40 minute packs on," Gerry pointed out.

The '40 minute' packs had two forty cubic feet of breathing air bottles. They were bulky, heavy, and cumbersome, theoretically supplying enough air for about 40 minutes, provided the user did not engage in strenuous physical activity. As far as Stan was concerned, even wearing one constituted strenuous physical activity. Those two guys would have to rotate, by hand, the 36 inch diameter hand wheel on the valve, probably 100 revolutions or more. The two operators climbed the ladder to the valve platform and, working one each side of the wheel, began to wrestle it closed. In about 20 minutes, the job was done. Gerry ordered the now isolated compressor vented to the flare, and the flame immediately decreased, sputtered, and finally died. The second H_2S emergency was over. The plant's bacon had been saved again, this time by two ordinary Cape Bretoners, just doing what they saw as their job.

B tower was put back into service a few days later. Some gas had been lost, the pressure had dropped somewhat, and the process seemed fairly stable. But one night a few days later, Stan was working late when Wayne, another of the shift supervisors, drifted into his office. "C tower level seems to be surging, and it's giving the stripper level control problems. I've called Dave," Wayne reported.

Stan wandered into the control room as Dave walked in, and watched as they got the instrument technicians to tune the level controller. The stench of H_2S filled the air as the ditch ran sour, and the panel operator hovered anxiously around the instrument technician, willing him to find the best settings quickly. Finally, the process calmed down, and Dave and Stan left together. "How come Wayne called you and not Rex?" Stan said conversationally. "I thought he was on call this week."

Dave glanced at him and gave a short, bitter, laugh. "You haven't noticed? Nobody calls Rex unless they have to. All you get is ranting and raving. Haven't you smelt his breath in the morning?"

Stan had to admit he had not noticed anything. But now he was intrigued, "You mean he's got a drinking problem?"

"I don't know what kind of a problem he has," Dave replied, "but nobody can get anything coherent out of him after about 6 o'clock."

"Have you spoken to Don?" Stan wanted to know.

"Don? Don't make me laugh. He thinks the sun shines out of Rex's rear end. Ever since Karl left, Rex has been the cat's meow. He's the only management guy here with any operating experience. Don won't do anything."

Stan drove home that night in a meditative mood, and for the first time in his life, couldn't sleep because of a work problem. What was going on here? Firstly, Dave's inability to go to Don with a problem like that boded ill for the management team. Stan was notoriously insensitive to personnel relation problems, and had noticed nothing wrong. Don could be very intimidating, and Dave would be wary of sidestepping his boss, Rex, not being sure how Don would respond. Dave was a new CGE employee, and could even fear losing his job. But anyway, it was none of Dave's business, was it? Stan awoke from a fitful sleep a few hours later with his mind racing. Suppose there was a bad incident at the plant, somebody was gassed, perhaps a member of the public, and CGE was sued? Stan's volatile imagination got to work as he pictured himself on the witness stand, "Now tell the jury, Mr. Davies. Were you aware that one of the management team had difficulties discharging his duties?" Hell, everybody had difficulties discharging their duties. But, Stan pondered, "What was his responsibility in a case like this?" Clearly, the proper course of action was to go to Don, which would take Dave off the hook. He could keep Dave out of it altogether. But, Dave had fingered the problem precisely. Stan wondered, "What would Don do in those circumstances, with no replacement for Rex on site? Probably nothing. And where would that leave Stan in his relationship with Don?"

Stan dozed off again, and woke up for breakfast with no answer in his mind. But driving in to work, a possible solution presented itself. "Dave was afraid to sidestep his boss, Rex. That was understandable. But what if he, Stan, sidestepped Don, and went right to Don's boss, CGE vice-president, Reg? That would get himself off the hook. Yeah, that would do it." He mentally reviewed his reply to the imaginary prosecuting council, "I viewed the situation seriously enough, sir, to advise the CGE vice-president of our division." That had a nice ring to it. What Reg did with the information was his responsibility.

So, that was precisely what Stan did. As soon as he got into work, he phoned Reg, who he had only met a few times, and really didn't know very well. Reg listened quietly, asked a few questions, and then reassured him, "Thanks for calling and telling me this, Stan. I know it wasn't easy. You've done the right thing. Leave it with me."

He put down the phone in a glow of self-righteousness, which quickly turned to uneasiness. "What had he done to Don? Don may have been a bit autocratic and remote, but he had always been fair to Stan. Did he deserve what had been done to him?" By the end of the day, Stan knew the answer was no, and there was only one way to put it right.

He marched into Don's office. "Don, I've got something to tell you." He told him what he had learned, without disclosing his source, and then, hanging his head, said, "I've called Reg and told him the same thing."

Don's response surprised him. "I wish you hadn't done that," he said quietly. Stan left his office thoroughly bemused. He wondered what was going on at the middle management levels.

A few days later, Don called all the management team into his office and said that he was resigning from CGE. Apparently, he had a very attractive offer from the Cape Breton Development Corporation, and, presumably, that was why he had not felt it necessary to reprimand Stan.

Reg came out from Toronto a few days later to announce the following management changes: Len was to be acting plant manager; Ted Bazely, a new guy from Ontario, would be Engineering Manager; and Stan was to be Production Manager, with Rex reporting to him. Stan was too immature, and too wound up in his own prospects and good fortune, to decline, although this particular outcome was the last thing he expected. Reg never mentioned that call to Stan, nor Stan to him. Stan should have said, "Look, Reg, I'm just a humble physicist, OK in the lab or for questions on process theory. What do I know of handling a bunch of unionized operators on shift? What do I know about emergency actions, life or death decisions, or protecting the community safety? Get someone else... give it to Dave." But, Stan said none of those things and accepted the Production Manager position.

All the shift supervisors, and even Rex, rallied around Stan with 200% support. Rex, although obviously disappointed, may have been secretly relieved. His personality could not take the pressure of the position he had been handed. Stan put him in charge of reviewing and revising the operating and emergency procedures, the documents which guided the shift supervisors and operators when any major change in process status became necessary, on either a planned or unplanned basis.

However, no amount of human support could disguise that the GS process was in trouble. Tower water levels and process flows could not be maintained at the values necessary for sustained production. Samples showed a tower to be producing on one shift, but not on the next. As the process deteriorated further, the decision was made in December to shut it down, and enter the towers to find out what was wrong.

The winter of 1970/71 turned out to be a bad one: howling gales, driving snow, and bitter wind chills. The worst of what Cape Breton had to offer. Like most chemical plants in those days, operators worked three eight-hour shifts, 8 am to 4 pm, 4 pm to 12 midnight, and midnight to 8 am. It was not always easy to get to work, especially at night, if the snow plows were off the road. The plant, of course, had its own snow removal equipment, both small motorized ploughs and shovels, as well as a giant backhoe with an enormous snow blade. On December 24th, a real Cape Breton blizzard began to blow. Most people went home early that afternoon, hoping their family had everything they needed for a Christmas day at home. A maintenance worker, let's call him Able, was working overtime that evening on the ploughs. About 10 pm that night, operator Baker, due to come in for the midnight shift, called his opposite number Charlie in the control room, "Man, Charlie, that's fierce out there tonight. What's going on?"

"It's pretty quiet in here tonight, Baker," Charlie said. "Thank God, the power plant seems to be OK. When are you going to be in? I was hoping to get home a bit early to help my wife."

"Well that's what I was really calling about," explained Baker. "There's one enormous snow drift across my drive, and we don't get many ploughs up here in the best of times. Even if I dug it out, I can't see how bad the rest of the road is. I'm not sure I can make it in. What's the road into the plant like? Aren't the other guys going to have the same problem? And how are you guys going to get home?" Baker lived not far away, in a mobile home park just on the edge of town.

There was more than one conversation along the same lines that night. The swing and night shift supervisors, exercising admirable judgement, decided that it was their duty to use the backhoe snow plough to keep the road into the plant open. The fact that it was not licensed for public road use was conveniently ignored. Nobody else was likely to be on the road that night anyhow. Precisely how the instructions to 'Keep access open to the plant' was transferred from the shift supervisor, to operator Charlie, to maintenance technician Able, is thankfully lost in the mists of time. Suffice to say, sometime between midnight and 5 am that Christmas morning, Santa Claus, in the form of the biggest snow plough seen in town for some time, appeared in Baker's modest mobile home park. There was not much room for the enormous backhoe in the park, and the driving snow did not improve the visibility. Nevertheless, Able cleared the roads in fine style. The problem began when, in an excess of Christmas spirit, Able decided to clear Baker's drive. This would have been a tight job for a six foot plough on a half-ton truck. For a twelve foot plough on a backhoe, it was next to impossible. The walls of a mobile home were like paper to such a machine, and with a crunch almost imperceptible in the cab; one of the backhoe outriggers caressed an adjacent home. Bakers' neighbor was not pleased by its impact. In a flash, Christmas spirit evaporated, and early on Christmas morning, the phone lines really began to hum.

But that was not all. That night, the blizzard, with its freezing temperatures, had begun to work its will on the plant. There were three large water block valves, now closed, which isolated the H_2S saturated water in the first stage towers from the stripper. Cunningly, the blizzard sought out the weakness in the heat tracing and insulation of these valves, and slowly hydrated the water in one of the bonnets. It did not have to work very hard, for the hydrate temperature was about 75 degrees Fahrenheit, child's play for a wind of 30 mph at about 0 degrees Fahrenheit. As the hydrate formed, like ice, it began to swell, slowly straining and stretching the bolts which held the valve bonnet to the body of the valve. About dawn, the wind abated, and the temperature rose slightly. Reinvigorated, the steam tracing rewarmed the valve bonnets. Soon, the hydrate melted, and H_2S laden water at 200 psi began to spray through the now useless bonnet seal. With the stench of gas permeating the site, and no obvious way of stopping the leak, the shift supervisor initiated an emergency call in, which reached Len shortly after the first call from the irate mobile home owner. His Christmas morning was not shaping up well at all.

Like a general marshaling his troops, Len sent Ted Bazely to deal with the fuming mobile home owner. Ted was our new maintenance manager, a tall, thin, somewhat stoop-shouldered mechanical engineer, a cheerful guy, seemingly completely imperturbable to the doings of man or machine. His job was just to fix it, whatever 'it' was.

Ted really pulled some fine strings that Christmas morning, after hitching a ride on a snowmobile he managed to calm down a seething citizen, who was threatening to sue CGE for everything they had. Despite his extreme anger, the damage was really quite minor, and the ultimate cost of repair was a paltry sum.

Meanwhile, in at the plant, Len and Stan's operations team reviewed their options. There were few good options. Since the towers were going to be emptied of gas anyway, the affected tower was 'flared', i.e. the gas in it was released to atmosphere via the flare. However much a relief it may have been to the shift supervisor, the sight of the flare tower flame was hardly a cheery Christmas sight.

But, it meant we had survived the first of the GS Christmas crises.

Through all the confusions and problems of that first production winter, the DW unit operated flawlessly, and 17 metric tons of product were produced, 68 big shiny 500 lb. stainless steel barrels of reactor grade heavy water. Under the terms of the contract, Atomic Energy of Canada was billed monthly, although the product was stored at the site until needed. At $20.50/lb, that represented almost $700,000 return on CGE's investment, which was already approaching $100 million. It was not very auspicious for the first year of production, and production was already one year late. The initial production run of the first large scale Canadian heavy water plant had lasted a little over three months. And Stan was presiding over a paper tiger, a GS unit still with the capability to kill, but without the wherewithal to earn its keep.

6 WHAT A MESS

Now there was a real problem. Remember hydrate, which would cause the H_2S saturated water to freeze at about 80 degrees Fahrenheit? This frightfully complicated process had to be shut down, and prevented from freezing, in a frigid Canadian winter. Moreover, at the same time, the gas had to be returned to storage, and the towers opened up to find out what was wrong. The first part was not too difficult; there was plenty of steam from the power plant, so the big vertical heat exchangers were put into the 'condensing' mode. This just meant the heat from the power plant steam was absorbed directly by the cooling tower, instead of the GS process. The resulting gigantic billows of steam were a feature of the site for the entire winter. At least there was a plentiful supply of warm water. The next crucial decision was how to deal with the H_2S. Since nobody knew what to expect, and there was the hope, mistakenly as it turned out, that production could resume soon, engineering elected to remove the gas from only one first stage tower at a time. The difficult part was 'isolating' the tower, that is making absolutely sure not the slightest trace of H_2S could leak from a part of the process which still had gas in it, into the tower which we intended to open. This involved a complicated process of 'venting and blanking', in which two valves would be closed, the space between them vented, and then a blank flange installed to absolutely block the gas path. There were, however, two huge 48" diameter gas pipes connecting each first stage tower to the second stage where this process was just not possible. Instead, the valves were 'double gate' valves, and the space between the two valve discs could be filled with pressurized oil. If the valves sealed properly, and if the oil filled space was maintained at a pressure above the gas pressure, no leak of deadly H_2S was possible. These were two big 'ifs', and the seal oil system was a constant worry to everyone through that first winter shutdown.

First, stage B tower was finally isolated in early January, 1972. The gas had already been flared, and the tower was 'steamed to flare', that is, steam was passed through the tower to sweep out residual H_2S. Next the tower was vented, and a small plume of steam began to emerge from the vent in the gas pipe at the very top of the tower, over 300 feet in the air. When that plume was declared H_2S free, the steam was shut off, allowing the tower to cool by drawing air in through the vent. Finally, the tower was ready to open, and maintenance technicians were dispatched to remove the manhole covers. At last, we got the first glimpse inside. The news was not good. At the bottom of the tower, where the big gas pipe entered from the compressor, several of the trays were destroyed. They had been forced, in some cases bent upward, then collapsed and swept aside by some unknown gale force emerging from the compressor pipe. At the middle of the tower, the damage was even worse. About 10 trays had disintegrated completely and even more trays above had sections missing. Major repairs would be required.

While engineering began to plan the necessary repair work, Stan's guys were wrestling with two questions. What had happened, and how could people safely work, for the extended periods which would obviously be necessary, inside those towers? Gerry put the second problem to Stan succinctly, "It's not so much the gas. I believe we've got that locked out, although you can never be too careful. But what if a guy gets ill in there, stroke, heart attack, or even breaks a leg? How do we even know to bring him help? And what if there is an emergency elsewhere on the plant - how do we let the guys in the tower know?"

With the aid of the safety supervisor, Tom, a system of safety monitors emerged. At each manhole where a work crew would enter, there must be an individual, remaining outside, whose job would be solely to communicate with the guys inside. If he needed help for someone in the tower, he could ring the 'Jesus Christ' alarm on that walkway. And if there was a plant gas emergency, it was his job to notify the guys inside, and count them as they came out. The job would not be pleasant. Maintenance intended to hire contractors and work two 10-hour shifts each day, seven days a week. The two hours between shifts would be for inspection of the work completed. So the poor guy hired as safety monitor would spend his entire shift, standing outside, up to 250 feet in the air, in the bitter wind of a Cape

Breton winter, night and day. It says much for the Cape Bretoner's fortitude, and desperate need for work, that there was only one problem with a safety monitor that entire winter.

Almost immediately, after the tower was opened for general inspection, Otto came in to see Stan. "Do you know the trays in the cold tower are almost completely plugged?" he questioned. Stan's heart sank. So that's where the Landrie Lake mud had been going! Mark brought some sample bottles and a flashlight, and off they hiked to the top manhole of B tower. Climbing inside, Otto's concern was clearly justified. The entire surface of the tray was covered with a dingy brown, slightly adherent deposit, somewhat like dried mud, perhaps an eighth of an inch thick. The gas holes were almost covered with a little mound of the stuff, usually with a tiny hole in the middle. Mark scraped a heap of it into his sample bottle. While Mark busied himself in the lab, Stan called Vic and described the scene.

Vic got very agitated. "Oh, my God, how could I have forgotten? I'll be right up."

Stan was mystified, "What had Vic forgotten?" Mark's preliminary analysis, and Vic, arrived in Stan's office about the same time the following day. "It seems to be 60-70% iron sulphide," Mark reported, "and the rest is probably organic."

Vic waved his hands in the air, as he did when he got excited, "Just as I thought, just as I thought! What is the concentration of iron in your feedwater?"

Stan was mystified again. "I don't know, we don't routinely

measure it, Stan admitted. "Mark, have you got any idea?"

"We do a complete raw water work up once a month, Mr. Davies. Let me check. I think it's about 2 parts per million," replied Mark.

Vic groaned, and then explained. "Iron sulphide is one of those comparatively rare compounds which suffer from 'reverse solubility' in water, meaning that as the temperature goes up, the iron sulphide becomes more, not less, soluble in water. Think about it, why does your kettle 'fur up' with calcium carbonate deposits? Because as you heat up the water, the amount of calcium carbonate which can be held in solution decreases, and the excess precipitates out, hence the scale on the bottom and around the electric heater. Now, raw, cold water is quite good at dissolving iron. Water isn't called 'the universal solvent' for nothing, and 2 parts per million of iron in water is not unusual. But the solubility limit of iron sulphide is only about 0.5 parts per million in the cold tower, so when H_2S saturated the water with sulphur, the iron sulphide precipitated out of solution, and onto the trays. At higher temperatures, the water can hold more iron sulphide in solution." The explanation was soon confirmed by an examination of other trays in the tower. All the cold trays were coated, but the hot trays were quite clean.

Now, engineering had a massive cleanup effort on their hands. Each tray was twenty-eight feet in diameter, and there were sixty-six of them in each of the three first stage towers, separated from their neighbors by eighteen inches. There was a manway in each tray, a rectangular, removable, bolted section about two feet long by one-and-a-half feet wide. With all these manways removed, there was a hundred foot shaft, right through the cold portion of the tower. Chemical cleaning was discussed, but the requisite acids could not be risked, nor could the use of high pressure hoses in the confined space. So to clean a tray, a man would have to enter through the nearest tower manhole and climb up, or down, the open manway shaft to his designated tray. Lying first on his back, he would have to scrub the tray above him with a wire brush until all the deposit was removed, then turn over onto his stomach and repeat the process for the tray on which he was lying. He would have to do this in half darkness and bitter cold. What a filthy job, but it was performed diligently and willingly by several work-starved Cape Bretoners.

Stan came in one clear, bitterly cold day, after a moderate snowfall the previous afternoon and evening, to find the night shift supervisor, Wayne, waiting for Dave and himself. "I had to relieve the safety monitor at B tower dehumidifier manhole. He was drunk," Dave reported.

"What did you do with him?" Stan asked.

"He's waiting downstairs in the lunch room."

"I suppose I'd better have a word with him." sniffed Stan.

Dave was incredulous. "Have a word with him? He's drunk and in charge of people's lives. What can he say? Let him go right now."

Stan hesitated, indecisive, but then made up his mind. "I can't fire a guy without hearing his side of the story," explained Stan. 'His' side of the story was simple. His shift was 8 pm to 8 am. About 6 pm, he got up, had supper, and dug his car out of the snow. When he tried to start it, he had no luck. He worked on it for a while, getting progressively colder, but still no luck. By now he knew he'd be late. Finally, he decided he had to walk out to the main road and hitch a ride into the plant. He hadn't 'been drinking', a Cape Breton euphemism for getting roaring, blinding drunk, but he had taken a small bottle of whiskey with him, "to help him keep warm on the walk out."

"How far is the walk from your house to the main road?" Stan asked.

"About two miles" was the reply.

That would be two miles over a rough forest track, Stan guessed, with about a foot of snow on it. He went back upstairs even more indecisive than when he went down. Here was a man who wanted work so badly he would walk two miles over a snow covered logging trail, in the hope of hitching a ride into town at 10 o'clock at night. Stan wasn't taken in by his 'small bottle' story. He had probably started to drink while trying to start the car, continued on the walk out, and on the ride into town. How he had concealed it from the supervisor who put him to work was anybody's guess, probably because the supervisor was so short of people that night. Stan knew he wouldn't have done what that man did to get to work. He'd have just phoned in and gone back to bed. "Was there even a phone?" He'd forgotten to ask.

Dave, now joined by Gerry, were both unimpressed, and turned thumbs down when Stan asked if he should be given another chance. To them it was simple black and white. A guy on safety duty must be sober - no ifs, ands, or buts. He could well be an alcoholic, and it would be an example to others. So Stan called Phil and told him to pay the poor guy off and dismiss him. There was no more trouble with safety monitors, and nobody else ever let them down.

Cape Breton had an endemic drinking problem, but Stan was slow to recognize it, even after the picnic fiasco. It was a long drive from D'Escousse, and he had begun to car pool with a local woman, Leona, who was a secretary at the plant. One Friday, she asked him a favor, "Mr. Davies, the husband of a friend of mine has got a temporary job at the plant, but he doesn't have a car. Can we give him a ride? He'll pay gas."

"Sure Leona," Stan replied. "It's my turn to drive next week. You can show me where he lives." The following Monday, Leona directed him to a tumble down house where he honked the horn. A small, grey, tired-looking man came down the drive, accompanied by a shabbily dressed woman and two even shabbier children. The whole family exuded poverty from every pore. But they proudly watched Dad get into the car and drive off to work, probably his first day's work in years. Paul was diffident to the point of almost not being present. He spoke only when directly questioned, and then most often with the shortest answer possible. He seemed pathetically grateful for the opportunity to work.

That Friday night, as Stan dropped him off, he offered $10, saying, "Thanks a lot, Mr. Davies. This is for the gas."

Even before the offer came, Stan had made up his mind. After seeing those children, he knew he could never live with himself if he accepted money from this man.

"I can't take that, Paul," he said, "I'd be driving into town anyway. Spend it on the kids." And he drove away, leaving Paul standing in the road with the ten dollar note in his hand.

Leona's thin, disproving lips became, if possible, even thinner. "You shouldn't have done that, Mr. Davies" she said disapprovingly.

"Oh come on, Leona. He needs that ten bucks far more than I do."

"You shouldn't have done it." she repeated stubbornly.

Stan let it pass, thinking she was worried about how it would look when she took the money next week. The following Monday morning, a silent Leona picked him up and drove straight past Paul's house.

"What's up, Leona? What about Paul?" Stan wanted to know.

"His wife came by this morning, Mr. Davies," she replied, eyes fixed on the road. "Paul isn't very well and can't go into work."

It took Stan most of the thirty minute drive to wheedle the real story out of her. It seemed Paul was so elated by his unexpected ten dollar bonus that he blew it at the local bootleg store on Sunday night and promptly drank himself into oblivion. Leona did her best to make Stan feel guilty. "I told you should have taken his money," she insisted severely.

There were many facets to Cape Breton drinking. Stan needed his car serviced, and about halfway between D'Escousse and Arichat was the only, somewhat dilapidated, GM dealer on the Island. Stan really wanted to use local services whenever he could, so he made a few cautious enquiries. His neighbor, Claude, was encouraging, but enigmatic. "Oh, that's run by George. He does good work. You'd better get it in before his next shutdown," Claude added.

Stan was puzzled. "You mean he takes shutdowns? How often?"

"About twice a year, usually spring and fall. Get it in before April and you'll be OK," said Claude.

So Stan took the plunge and made an appointment. When he dropped the car off, George was all efficiency, "That's no problem, Mr. Davies. It should be ready Friday night."

"Fine. Give me a call and I'll pick it up," said Stan.

George wouldn't hear of it. He insisted, "No, No, I'll drop it at your place." True to his word, Friday night George returned a smoothly running car.

Stan asked him to step inside as he wrote out the check, "Thanks a lot, George. Can I offer you a drink?"

George seemed surprised. "No thank you, Mr. Davies. I'm not drinking just at the moment. But if I see you in April, I'll take you up on that offer." It turns out that George's 'shutdowns' were his two week holidays, which, it seemed, he passed in a state of cheerful inebriation. Between times, he wouldn't touch a drop.

Just cleaning the trays didn't solve the plant's bigger problem. How could the plant ever run again if the raw water had too much iron? Obviously, some water treatment was required to clean up the feedwater. The standard technique, called clarification, is almost certainly used, in some variant, for the water piped into your house. It works like this. Alum, or aluminum sulphate, $Al2SO4$, is highly soluble in water. Aluminum hydroxide is almost completely insoluble.

So if you add alum and caustic soda, NaOH, a precipitate of Al2(OH)3 forms. The process is called 'coagulation', and the precipitate is 'floc', another pair of slippery slinky glutinous words from science which sound vaguely like the process they describe. You can try it on your kitchen countertop if you've got the raw materials. The precipitate which forms is a fluffy, spidery, hairy, filamentous substance, with two important properties. Firstly, it tends to stick to other things in the water and helps other compounds to precipitate out of solution also. Equally importantly, it can be filtered out of the water by a simple sand bed filter of the type already installed at the plant. The process is normally carried out in a large tank, called a clarifier.

The trouble was, putting in a clarifier, was expensive and a long term proposition, which couldn't possibly be done in a month or two. Leo, and our consultant, Larry Hopkins from the Dearborn Company who supplied our water treatment chemicals, hit on the idea of adding the chemicals at the Landrie Lake pumphouse. The chemical reaction, which is not very fast, could then go on in the pipeline as the water travelled from the pumphouse to the plant. The first experiments were a comedy of errors. The alum and caustic soda were pumped from old oil drums. They were supposed to be added in carefully controlled, precisely measured, 'parts per million' quantities, but that was impossible. Like your mother's cooking, a handful of this and a dash of that had to do. And Dearborn had a brand new, high tech, 'coagulant aid'. This was a long chain polymeric molecule, which, when dissolved in water, became strongly ionized, that is electrically charged. It then attached itself to the microscopic particles of insoluble aluminum hydroxide, and drew them together to form the desired 'floc' more quickly. It was to be added, so the laboratory tests said, in even more microscopic 'tenths of a part per million'. When dry, the product was a slightly granular white powder. Unfortunately, the first delivery of a few pounds of the stuff got damp somewhere between Halifax airport and Landrie Lake. At the lake, Leo and Larry were faced with a solid gelatinous mass, which they had to attack with shovels to dissolve a roughly measured portion in an old oil drum. Despite all the problems, the initial experiments improved the water quality dramatically. 'In-line flocculation' had been invented, and it worked quite well, up to a point. The iron in solution was reduced below the magic figure of 0.5 parts per million, and most of the silt was cleaned out of the feedwater. There were two disadvantages. First, the equipment was off-site, but had to be tended by our operators when chemicals had to be received, or adjustments made. Second, all the silt was now being removed in our filters, a job for which they had not been designed.

During this long, unproductive and frustrating second winter, management and supervisory relationships with the hourly paid personnel seemed to worsen, for no obvious reason. In fact, on Stan's side of the house, things were never very bad. The operators were not exactly balls of fire, and getting the essential minimum of work out of them was never very easy, especially on the night shift. But, by and large, they were easy going, could be brave and resourceful, as has already been seen, and seemed prepared to cooperate with management. But on the maintenance side of the plant, which bore the brunt of the unpleasant jobs that winter, a mood of conflict was spreading. It was no surprise when a union began to organize, and soon thereafter the Oil, Chemical & Atomic Workers were certified to represent workers at the plant. Several supervisors were relieved that one of the more militant Cape Breton coal mining unions was not represented. Later, a three year agreement was negotiated with very generous hourly pay rates. A number one operator, with his 42 hour week and shift differential, would earn substantially more than some of the engineers, a fact that those same engineers were not slow in calling to management's attention. The agreement was back dated to the previous summer, so in theory there were two more years of industrial peace to go. However, not many supervisors were to characterize the next two years that way.

By about late February, B tower was cleaned and repaired. It was to be put back into service, even though no product could be produced with only one first stage tower. But operating it was judged to be safer than leaving it shutdown. The operators would gain experience, and the embryonic water treatment could be tested. So the same steps taken to free the tower of gas were implemented in reverse, steaming it out to get rid of the air, removing the isolation, and finally pressure testing all of the equipment prior to reintroducing H_2S. In the last stages of this process, routinely pressure testing one of the banks of heat exchangers with water, they would not hold pressure. "Oh, oh," you could hear people thinking, "What now?"

The problem was worse than anyone envisaged. These heat exchangers were simple 'tube in shell' devices, that is, one part of the water or steam flowed through hundreds of stainless steel tubes, while the other part of the water or steam flowed over the outside of the same tubes, in the 'shell' of the exchanger. Heat was transferred from the hotter side to the colder. They were designed so that the entire bundle of tubes could be removed from the shell, no easy task when you remember a tube bundle was sixty feet long, up to four feet in diameter, and weighed many tons. When we finally got a bundle out of its shell for inspection, we were horrified to find it had cancer. Well, not really, but cancer is a very appropriate description of the pitting corrosion which had afflicted all the tubes. Each tube was, of course, covered with a fine film of our Landrie Lake mud. When this was washed off, at intervals along a tube, small round discolored pits could be seen. Some of these pits had penetrated so deeply into the one-tenth of an inch thick metal, that there was a small round hole right through the wall of the tube.

The cause of this problem was not hard to trace, but, like almost every problem on our plant, it was not as simple as it seemed at first sight. It soon transpired that only half of our big heat exchangers were so afflicted, while the other half were OK. The ones which were OK were made out of a type of stainless steel called '316L', while the ones with cancer were made out of '304L', these numbers representing two different specifications for stainless steel. The 'L' just stood for low carbon. 304 was an old specification which had been around for many years, while 316 was a newer, supposedly better, specification introduced in the 1960's. At the time the plant was designed, the main concern about the use of stainless steel was stress corrosion cracking in H_2S service. The use of low carbon steel was known to prevent stress corrosion cracking, and was therefore mandatory on the plant. Hence, the 'L' designation was specified in both cases. While 316 steel was more corrosion resistant than 304, it was also, of course, much more expensive. The DuPont Savanah River plant, having been designed and built before 316 steel was available, used only 304L, and had no real stress corrosion problems. Don and Len had used the best metallurgical advice available, and their consultants had not been able to find any reason favoring the more expensive 316 stainless steel in H_2S service. Therefore, Don compromised and selected 316L for what he thought were the more severe duties in the plant, and used the cheaper 304L elsewhere. Now, with hindsight being 100% better than foresight, it was obvious the wrong question had been asked. The corrosion actually experienced was due to chloride pitting, in which a salt concentration built up under the Landrie Lake mud. The 316 stainless steel was, unlike 304, specifically formulated to resist chloride attack.

So there was no choice but to 'retube', in technical parlance, almost half of the giant heat exchangers. This meant removing the tube bundle, itself no small task, from each of a dozen heat exchanger shells, and shipping each bundle to Montreal. There, Dominion Steel dismantled each bundle, rebuilt it with new 316L tubing, and shipped it back to us, to be reinstalled in its shell. The old tubing was sold for scrap, to eventually become lawn furniture, a nice twist, "GS to Grass", as somebody said.

Now, Ted really showed his strengths as maintenance manager, and dealt with the logistics like a military campaign. Stan expected the plant to be shut down for about six months. It says a lot for Ted, his crew of maintenance engineers and technicians, CN railways, and the Montreal factories, that the job was completed much more quickly. In the end, removing a tube bundle to reinstalling it took about two weeks and since a second bundle could be removed while waiting for the first to be returned, so the whole campaign took only about three months. Although Stan was used to the English pace of dealing with the unexpected, namely very slowly and carefully, this was a fine demonstration of Canadian 'can-do' team spirit. By late April, the plant was almost ready to start up again. However, there was one more lesson in Cape Breton psychology to come.

The 450 foot flare tower had two bright red aircraft warning lamps, both of which had failed. Replacing them was almost the last job before start up. It meant taking the elevator to the top platform, walking along the top walkway, climbing about 150 foot of stairs, ascending the last 50 feet in a caged ladder, and carrying the necessary lamps and tools. To make the task more difficult, breathing equipment had to be worn at the top. Actually, there was really no risk that a gas release to the flare tower would occur. If it did, no amount of breathing equipment would save you from being fried to a crisp by the flame. But, there was known to be both nitrogen and

H_2S in the flare, either of which could asphyxiate you, and the breathing equipment would have to be worn right at the top while the simple lamp replacement job was carried out.

It was almost three o'clock on a dull, miserable, breezy, Friday afternoon, with a hint of rain in the air, when Stan heard the flare job had been postponed until Monday. He called the maintenance supervisor up to his office. "What's going on, Jim," he asked. "We can't start up tomorrow unless you get those lamps replaced. We'll lose at least three days. What's the problem?"

"Can't get the guys to go up," Jim responded, "The wind is beginning to blow and they say it's too dangerous."

Stan protested, "Might be worse Monday. We can't have your guys deciding what's dangerous and what isn't, or we'll never get this plant into production. The whole job's permitted, tagged and ready to go."

Jim looked at Stan speculatively, "Would you be prepared to do it?"

"Of course," Stan replied. "Normally, I quite like climbing the flare tower. Not especially in this weather, but I'd do it to get the plant going again."

"OK. Get suited up and meet me downstairs. The guys are on their afternoon break." Jim walked out.

Stan swallowed, and began to heave on his outside gear and breathing equipment. He had never climbed the flare tower with breathing equipment, and certainly never in this weather. But his bluff had been called, and damn it, he did want to start up this weekend. He met Jim downstairs and they topped up their air cylinders. Jim led Stan into the so-called lunchroom. It was crowded with about 50 dirty, sweaty men wearing overalls. The buzz of conversation died down as they entered. Jim looked round to find the man he wanted. "Hey, Joe," said Jim conversationally, "Where are those flare tower lamps? Stan and I are going up the flare to replace them." A pin could have been heard drop in the breathless silence as Joe looked them both up and down.

"It's getting mighty windy out there," said Joe, "and dark too."

"Yeah. But we just have to get those flare lamps fixed to start up," explained Jim.

There was another expectant pause. Then Joe sighed heavily, "I guess if they're that important to you, Bob and I'll do it after we've had this cup of coffee."

"Thanks, Joe," said Jim breezily, and they sauntered out. Jim almost doubled up, trying not to laugh.

"What's so funny?" Stan asked. "I thought you said they wouldn't do it?"

"They wouldn't. Not for me. But don't you see. You challenged their manhood. If I had said I was going to do it, there would have been all sorts of problems, discussions, grievances. But when management appears, and is ready to go where they won't, that's a different story. Can't let management imply you're scared."

"So you had me on," said Stan, "You knew we weren't going up?"

"Well, I was fairly sure," mused Jim. "But, you can never tell with this lot. We might have found our own bluff called. Would you have gone up?"

"Of course," replied Stan breezily.

The plant restarted conservatively, at the low pressure of about 200 psi of H_2S. Apart from a few minor problems with the new off-site water treatment, the plant ran beautifully, and everyone began to heave cautious sighs of relief as production, or rather extraction, began to exceed 50%.

So, what is the difference between extraction and production? Extraction is what was being taken out of the feedwater, and production is what was going into drums and what the customer was billed for. Let's do some simple arithmetic. In that beautiful May and June of 1971, there might have been about 2.5 million pounds of feedwater every hour, each pound going into the process with 147 parts per million of deuterium, and the same pound leaving with 121 parts per million. So the GS process was extracting 147-121 or 26 times 2.5, which is about 65 pounds per hour of precious product. That was also, of course, 65% of the design extraction rate. But at the money end, the DW unit, there might be only two drums a day, say about 40-45 pounds per hour. This was production. So, where was the difference going? Why, into inventory in the process of course. By that summer, there were about 20 tons in inventory. The good news was, when inevitable equipment problems, such as a faulty pump, compressor, or valve, shut down one of the first stage towers for a few days, the DW unit would continue on its merry way, producing at the same 42 pounds per hour. The bad news was, not only would the extraction have to be increased to the design figure of 100 pounds per hour, but also all the equipment must be kept running, at least 8000 hours out of a possible 8760 in a year.

However, even 42% production was not to be sneezed at, especially after what everyone at the plant had been through in the last twelve months, and Cape Breton was a glorious place to be in the summer. Stan had his speedboat back in the water, and the family was learning to water ski. The kids picked it up as though they were born to it. His eldest daughter got so good she would walk to the beach fully clothed... as fully clothed as a teenager ever was during a Cape Breton summer..., kick off her shoes, step into the skis, and be off like the wind, fair hair streaming behind her. After a while, satisfied, and letting the rope go, she would ski back onto the beach, still dry. A Saturday or Sunday afternoon was sure to find a gaggle of village kids on the dock, wistfully watching the Upper Canadians enjoy themselves. Inevitably, Stan's youngsters would insist that their friends be given a turn. So he taught his two eldest children how to steer the boat, and soon he could relax on the dock with a beer, like a true Cape Bretoner, watching the kids enjoy themselves.

When the tide was high, the preferred method of entry was to sit on the dock and, as the rope tightened, jump into the water only a couple of feet below your skis. If the practitioner was skilled, this could also be done fully clothed. Canada was not a litigious society, and Stan gave little thought to the risks involved, until the day his son Raymond, aged 14, was piloting the boat for a friend about the same age. The friend wanted to learn the 'jump from the dock' entry method. The lad sat on the dock side and took a firm grip on the tow rope, while Raymond maneuvered to take up the slack.

Unfortunately, Raymond gunned the throttle while there was still slack in the rope, and the boat took off with a roar. The surprised novice skier was jerked horizontally through the air before he could let go. Opening his mouth to shout, or scream perhaps, he entered the water face first, and took a large mouthful of sea water. Cape Breton youngsters were as tough as their parents, and he seemed none the worse for wear when he was fished, gasping, out of the Atlantic. Stan re-qualified Raymond as a tow boat operator, but noticed his friend was content to sit on the sidelines.

Stan and his family got a lot of fun out of their boat. Sometimes they would load the kids up, those who wanted to come, and take off down the beautiful Lennox Passage, for a day and a picnic on the beach. This particular Sunday, with his wife and two of the four children, Stan decided to cross the passage, about 5 miles, and explore the coast on the Cape Breton side. It was a beautiful sunny day, and the sea sparkled invitingly. Leaving the jetty, he opened up the throttle and the boat leapt forward, generating a foaming wake on the calm surface. A few minutes later, he slowed and entered the twisting Bourgeoise Inlet. Raising the outboard engine, the family drifted in to shore, and dragged the boat up onto the sand. Returning a few hours later, Stan noticed some children playing with the steering wheel, but they ran off when he shouted. He inspected the boat, but could find no damage, other than the steering cable which had unwound from the steering drum. Cursing, he laid on his back with the hull ribs digging painfully into his back, while he rewound it.

Their traditional boat launch procedure was to have Joy at the sharp end, while he pulled out to sea with a paddle. When the water was deep enough, the outboard could be lowered and started. Today, the tide was ebbing fast. "OK Joy" Stan instructed, "We'll be swept downstream pretty quickly here. I don't want to ground on that little headland. As soon as I've got the engine in, let 'er rip and let's get some steerage way on her. Do you want to take her home, if it's as calm as when we came?"

A few yards off shore Stan lowered the engine. "Let's go," he bellowed, and the engine obediently coughed into life and steadied to a healthy roar.

"Not that way!" he roared, as the boat curved in towards the beach. "What are you doing?" The boat curved the other way.

"There's something wrong with the steering!" screamed Joy.

"Here, let me have it," Stan said scathingly, leaping forward. "What can possibly be wrong with the steering? When you turn the wheel, the engine pivots, just like it's supposed to." He soon found out. Rewinding the steering cable from underneath, he had wound it backwards. Now when the wheel was turned to the left, the boat steered to the right! "Damn! What a nuisance," he complained. Should he return to the beach and fix it? Nah, it would be only a few minutes to get home, and he could fix it easier tied up at the jetty. In fact, it was rather fun, when you got the hang of it.

Laughing, Stan opened the throttle and rounded the headland. My God, what was this? Two foot waves in a channel so narrow he could not turn around, even if the steering was normal. He throttled back, keeping enough speed on the boat to maintain steering. The current swept them towards the open sea. Perhaps this was just a tidal current. But no, further out to sea the waves increased. Where was that serene ocean they had crossed just a few hours before? Now it was grey, turbulent, and menacing. Where had this wind come from? They hadn't felt it in the channel. Now the waves were so big he dare not take them head on. And he must remember the reversed steering. He set a heading at about a forty-five degree angle to the direction of the waves, and the little craft began a wallowing, purposing motion out to sea. He risked a glance backward. No sign of the channel, only 3-4 foot waves racing towards a rocky shore. The boat was beginning to take on water when he did not ride a wave at the correct angle. He forced himself to think.

"Joy, make sure all the kids have their life jackets on properly and securely. We'll head west down the channel, try to get in the lee of Isle Madame. Here we're directly exposed to that south-easterly wind which seems to have come from nowhere. Further up, perhaps we can cross. I think we'll be OK, but who knows what the waves are like out in the channel. And grab that bailer and don't let any water accumulate. I want to keep her riding high."

Sure enough, after a mile or so of heading west, either the waves diminished or, just as importantly, Stan was getting used to them. He turned across the channel, and soon the waves began to subside. By the time they entered D'Escousse Bay, on the lee shore of Isle Madame, the water was the same calm, inviting, sparkling ocean they had set out on that morning. Tying up, he hauled himself up on the jetty and looked back towards where they had spent the afternoon.

From here, Cape Breton drowsed pleasantly in the afternoon sun, giving no inkling of the treacherous conditions on that windward shore. He had been given a sharp lesson, but worse, he had unknowingly risked his family. For that, he could never forgive himself.

But leisure is fleeting, and work is eternal. The plant production rate must be increased. The pressure in the GS process, and the gas and water flows were systematically increased. Soon, the sand filters could not stand the load. Each of the eight filters was designed to 'backwash' automatically on a timed cycle. Backwashing was just what its name implied; water flowed backwards through the filter to rid it of its load of accumulated mud and silt, deposited in it by the improvised method of water clarification. Each filter had, of course, to be taken out of service while this was in progress, and the remaining seven filters then had to absorb the full water flow. At such times, water would spout into the air from the vent pipes, as the pressure across the dirtiest filters increased. The feedwater flow could not be increased further until more permanent water treatment was installed, and the decision was soon taken to install a clarifier designed specifically for our needs. The design and installation of this critical piece of equipment took all summer and most of the fall.

Having some of the plant operating equipment off-site provided an opportunity too good to miss. At least once each shift, the water treatment operator had to get a truck, drive to Landrie Lake pumphouse, and perform cursory inspection of the pumps and chemical tanks. Less frequently, he might also have to make a process adjustment, to alter the amount of chemicals being added to the water stream, or help to unload a alum tanker of its cargo. These were heaven sent opportunities to get away from the prying eyes of supervision and the heavy hand of management. One late spring night shift, dispatched on a routine visit just before dawn was breaking, an operator, who shall be nameless, had a bright idea. Why not get in a bit of duck hunting? With a companion, and their shotguns, he drove the half ton company truck, not to the pumphouse, but up a logging road to his favorite spot on the lake, and waited for the sun to rise. Later, the miscreants returned to the truck, only to get it stuck in the mud. They radioed the plant for help as the morning shift change began, and were soon joined by a ten ton truck, which also got stuck. Now management got involved, demanding to know why the water treatment chemistry had not been adjusted as per laboratory specifications.

"Man, that road to the lake is real bad this time of year!" was the control room operator's response as he arranged for the large backhoe to succor the growing band of cheerful duck hunters.

Meanwhile, Stan suffered a severe personnel blow. Doug gave in his notice; he was going to work for a computer service in Montreal. Stan conferred with Len. "Len, I don't think this operation is going to be as simple as Vic would have us believe. I'm losing my only guy who's really up on the theory of the process, and I'm sure water quality is going to be a constant problem for us. I'd like to hire a top notch chemical process engineer, and a dedicated water chemist."

Len gave his OK, and advertisements were placed in the Globe and Mail. The response was disappointing in quantity, but the quality was good. Cape Breton was not a desirable location to many professional engineers. Engineers who were born in Canada, of course, had not bothered to reply, but recent immigrants were plentiful. And so Shin-der Chang and Gordon Portway joined Stan's staff.

Shin-der was a Chinese Nationalist, a fugitive from Communism, and a PhD in Chemical Engineering. Unable to get an engineering job, he was eking out a living at Ottawa University. His command of English was very good, but his pronunciation was terrible. Fortunately, Stan decided that since he would be communicating with others mainly through writing and numbers, his lack of language skills could be ignored. That was a lucky decision, since he was to be instrumental in saving the plant's bacon later.

Gordon was an Australian chemist, with some experience in water purification, touring the world as Australians like to do. He had come to North America via Los Angeles that summer, and flown to Canada in the fall. Los Angeles in the summer was very similar to his native country, dry, parched and brown. He arrived in Toronto just after an early snowstorm had covered the countryside in white. Stan recruited him at once, and he arrived in a snow-covered Cape Breton, just in time for the commissioning of the clarifier. The following spring, he was to be amazed at the lush Nova Scotian vegetation. "Ain't it green," was all he could say, "Ain't it green." In his world travels so far, he had completely skipped green grassy fields.

It was an early winter that year, and the weather was already freezing as the clarifier was commissioned on December 1st. It was piped up so that it could start up on-line, that is without shutting down the plant. Startup was relatively smooth and problem-free. The clarifier took out 90% of the silt, which the filters had been removing. As the clear water replaced the muck previously going to the filters, you could almost hear them sigh with relief as the burden was lifted from their shoulders. Now the filters could revert to their normal, 'polishing' function, that is removing the residual floc from the water leaving the clarifier. Stan's staff mentally girded their loins. There was now nothing to prevent full production! The GS pressure had been held down to about 220 psi through the summer, but now it could be raised. Mindful of last winter's fiasco, it was taken only to 240 psi, and about 75% extraction reached before the next disaster hit.

In mid-December, Landrie Lake turned over. As water is cooled, like most liquids, it gets denser, that is a given volume weighs more. So the water at the top of the lake, cooled by the rapidly cooling air above, sinks to the bottom, displacing warmer water to the top, to be cooled in its turn. If this kept going right down to freezing, the lake would freeze solid, and all the fish would die. But water has a funny property. At a few degrees above freezing, it has its maximum density, and as it is cooled further, it gets less dense, so the cold water stays on top. Eventually a skim of ice forms on the top, and as it thickens as the winter draws on, the little fishes are safe underneath. This is what is often referred to as 'the fish's life-line.'

The trouble in Landrie Lake began just before it froze. As the convection currents roiled the waters, some unknown and unmeasurable change occurred. There was little apparently wrong with the process conditions; water flowed to the towers, the gas circulated, and superficially everything seemed OK. But evidence indicated that considerable amounts of water were being 'entrained', that is the gas flow leaving the top of the tower carried large quantities of water with it. Process samples indicated the first stage tower extraction was decreasing. Mindful of the damage caused to the trays in the bottom of the tower the previous year, gas and liquid flows were progressively reduced.

By Christmas, the process was stabilized again, at about sixty percent extraction, just about the same level achieved most of the summer, without a clarifier. Had all that expense been for nothing? Reviewing the second year of production, there was little cause for celebration. The GS process had run for only seven of the twelve months, and for much of that time, not all the equipment had been operable. To be sure, some of the down time was attributable to the power plant, but much of it could be laid directly at the door of the heavy water plant and its staff. The design production rate of the plant was 100 pounds per hour, and allowing for 760 hours of down time, production should be 400 metric tons per year. Barely 40 metric tons had been produced in 1971. Even allowing for the five months of shut down, the plant had produced at only about a quarter of its design rate, pretty miserable and far from a profitable level. Moreover, one of the big 500MWe CANDU power plants at Pickering, Ontario, was completed, but could not start up for lack of heavy water. It needed about 500 tons of the stuff. Nobody knew how much heavy water Atomic Energy of Canada had in storage, but the Port Hawkesbury Heavy Water Plant contribution was obviously pitifully small. The phone lines from AECL to CGE must have been humming. How long would CGE management let the current team continue to stumble around?

7 BIG BROTHERS

The first part of that second winter found the operators worrying more about the weather, and just keeping the plant on line, rather than about perfecting extraction. It was bitterly cold, with frequent high winds and temperatures twenty to thirty below freezing, producing vicious wind chills. And heaven help the man who had to climb the towers for samples or instrument problems. One particularly biting day, the level indication on C tower began to behave erratically. A bundled up instrument technician was sent out to check the transmitter, the electronic package which transmitted the signal to the control room panel. As he returned to the control room, blowing on his hands and pronouncing the transmitter OK, B tower level began to exhibit the same behavior. Now things were getting serious, and the control room operator began to hover over the all-important stripper level indication. If that went, a spot decision would have to be taken whether to shut down the plant. And if shut down in this weather, who knew when it might be running again?

"Those damn level static lines have got to be hydrating," fumed Dave. "Check the steam tracing again." The level transmitters just measured the pressure difference between the water in the bottom of the tower and the gas above it. The static lines were two inch diameter pipes leading from the tower to the level transmitter. They held H_2S saturated water on one side, and H_2S gas on the other, and were called 'static' because the gas and the water was stationary. For this reason, they were prone to freeze, and had a half inch steam tracing line strapped to them, under the thick insulation. The steam tracing line, soon pronounced OK by a frozen field operator, would be at about 350 degrees Fahrenheit. If the insulation was OK, and the steam tracing was OK, how could the static line possibly be chilled to 85 degrees Fahrenheit?

Soon, a shivering Otto came into the control room. With his characteristic thoroughness, he had dug out the appropriate drawings showing how the static lines were designed, and had then gone out to see for himself. "The static line is braced to some structural steel by a thick metal clamp," he announced. "That clamp is attached directly to the static pipe and directly to the structural steel, and it is only a few inches long. I bet that is where it's hydrating." Otto was right. The structural steel, being so cold and exposed to the elements, was sucking heat through that metal clamp like soda through a straw, and the end of the clamp attached to the pipe was cooler than 85 degrees. Operators were sent out to insulate the clamp, steam hoses were wrapped round the adjacent structural steel, and the level indicators resumed their normal indications. As a precaution, a steam hose was also wrapped around the stripper level static line.

So that crisis was overcome, but a few days later the weather struck again, this time from a different quarter. It was a cold, snowy, windy night, and the weekly poker game had been under way for some time at the company house. The phone rang, and after a few minutes, Dave, who was on call, came back to the table, looking puzzled. "Jim says they can't keep the cooling tower water level up. It's dropping steadily, but the pumping station says they are OK and the head tank level is normal. I suppose we'd better go and have a look," said Dave.

Dave, Gerry and Stan bundled up and climbed into the emergency vehicle, fortunately a four wheel drive. Dave believed that a four wheel drive gave one a great feeling of security in Cape Breton. And that night they were to need it. They drove through the blinding snow, a mile past the plant, and turned up the dirt road to the lake. At the pumping station, the lone operator was co-operative. "That head tank level has hardly moved all night," he said, "but, you guys can't be using much water. I've been cutting back all evening, and now I'm down to only one pump. Normally I'll keep three going for you."

Dave sighed, "I suppose we'll have to go and have a look at the head tank. Come on." So, climbing back into the Jeep, the Three Musketeers started out. The track alongside the pipe line was rough, pitch dark, and narrow, with no room to turn the Jeep around. The snow seemed to be falling heavier. At intervals, there were large frozen puddles from the water spurting from the leaking wood stave pipe. In the four wheel drive, they bumped, slipped and fought their way for half a mile to the top of the hill between the lake and the plant where the head tank was located. Reaching the clearing, Dave left the head lights shining on the tank, and everyone got out to prowl around. The head tank was quite small, perhaps thirty feet in diameter and about the same in height. From here, the water pipe ran underground, downhill into the plant.

"I can't tell if there's any water in it," Dave grumbled, "Anybody got any ideas?"

Gerry climbed the small ladder and wrestled open a loose manhole on the domed top. "I can hear water running," he reported. "Bring me up a flashlight." He shone it down into the cavernous blackness. "I still can't see anything. Toss me up a stone." He dropped a large round stone into the tank. There was no splash, only a resounding thud as it hit bottom.

"The damn tanks empty," Gerry raged, "I'll bet their level indicator is frozen, and that dumb ass operator has been cutting back the water flow all night, thinking his tank is full. It is no wonder Jim can't get enough water." Carefully reversing the Jeep, they retraced their path, and, not exactly politely, explained the problem to the pump house operator.

"I don't care if your ******** head tank does overflow," Dave told a crestfallen pump house man, "Run all your pumps until our cooling tower basin is full. Then run as many as you normally do until you can get that level indicator fixed."

By the time they got back to the house, it was 1.30 am and still snowing.

"I'm not driving 30 miles to D'escousse in this weather. I'll stay here for the night," Stan told Gerry. He did not phone his wife, expecting her to be asleep, and not wishing to wake her. He should have known better. A light sleeper, she woke about 2.30 am. Finding Stan not by her side, and convinced he was either in the ditch somewhere, or worse, in somebody else's bed, she woke up half of Port Hawkesbury before locating him. This was a source of considerable ribald amusement to the poker game participants, although the wives who were disturbed, seemed not to share the joke. Such was a typical winter's night in Port Hawkesbury.

Soon, the blow that everyone been dreading fell. Len called the management staff into his office and announced he had received a call from Reg. A new plant manager and a new operations manager had been retained. They were to join the plant soon. Reg was leaving the organization to the new manager, so Len and Stan were left gnawing their fingernails until the new men arrived. The new managers were both experienced in chemical plant operations, being from the large Canadian chemical producer, Polymer Corporation. Thus, came into being the period referred to as 'the polymerization of CGE'. Polymerization is the process by which, in certain plastics, molecules are joined together. Although sourly humorous, the phrase was more prescient than anyone could foretell. The plant and its diverse workers would indeed be fused into a single homogeneous team structure by one of the new managers.

Lee Dugan, the new plant manager, arrived first. He certainly had been good looking in his younger days, and still retained a rugged, handsome appearance, even though he was obviously in his sixties. Of average build, although somewhat stocky, he adjusted his demeanor to the needs of the situation. When seeking information, he was courteous, charming (said Joy), but persistent. Faced with confrontation, real or imagined, he would assume a pugnacious attitude, legs slightly apart, hands in pockets, shoulders hunched forward. Sensing a fellow straight shooter, Stan liked him at once. After closeting himself with Len, Lee held a management meeting devoted to his background. The Polymer Corporation had been created by the Canadian government in World War II for the express purpose of making synthetic rubber. They had obviously had their share of problems with novel processes, since they had rapidly scaled up from prototype to full scale production to meet the exigencies of the war. Lee had risen with the growth of the new company, retiring recently as a vice-president of operations. He stated frankly that he did not consider his present position to be permanent; he would only be here long enough to get the plant up to full production. Len would continue as his deputy. That raised some eyebrows, since the title 'deputy' was unknown in GE and CGE, corporate philosophy holding that there was either a real job that needed doing, or there wasn't. No half measures.

Lee was an old hand at plants in trouble. If this was typical, he knew he could expect one of three things, alone or in combination: poor morale, poor management, or union problems. Technical problems, in his experience, were seldom long lasting. Just turn the engineers loose, and the poorly performing piece of equipment would soon be located and fixed or replaced. Lee soon found that at this plant, he was facing all three, and something more. At the professional level, morale was not good. The engineers, and even local management, had a sense of isolation from the Toronto head office, real or imagined. Local professionals thought that nobody from Upper Canada knew what it was like to live and work in Cape Breton, unless they had been there. Also, their Toronto management, while highly critical of the plant financial performance and demanding improvement, seemed to spend precious little time on site, understanding the real problems of keeping a plant of this size and complexity just operating, let alone improving its output. Management was not so much poor, as inexperienced in the job which needed to be done. Motivation, follow through, measurement, discipline, were all skills which, in Lee's eyes, needed improvement. And union relations were clearly deteriorating rapidly. Lee had not yet got the measure of these Cape Bretoners, but he already sensed they were a breed apart. And then, Lee contemplated, "Just what was wrong with the plant? Why did it work almost as designed some times, and then have to be cut back?" Nobody seemed to know.

Lee knew all these problems could be dealt with, given time and money. He dealt with the last problem, and in his experience the most unusual, first. At a private meeting, he told Stan that when the new operations manager arrived, he was to be relieved of all operations responsibilities, and given the task of finding out what was wrong with the process. He could select his own team from anyone on site. Back in his office, Stan shut the door and pondered. Demoted, by God! But he had to admit the logic of the decision. In practice, Dave had been doing most of the operations manager job. Stan was not skilled in human or union relations, knew little of the personnel problems in running shift operations, and was not normally of much use in emergency situations. On the other hand, by now he knew as much as anyone about how the process should work, and had the interest and technical knowledge to find out why it didn't. Moreover, Reg had contacted the GE corporate research and development laboratory at Schenectady, New York, a world renowned operation. They were also going to put together a team to help, and Stan would be the interface. Lee had not mentioned any reduction in salary. His spirits rose. And thus came into existence the famous, or infamous, depending on your point of view, 'Port Hawkesbury Foaming Task Force.'

There was one residual personnel problem which Stan had to clear up before ceding his operation to new management. And that was Mark. As the plant problems developed, so did Mark's. Stan's inability to bring the plant production level up to design became, through Mark's intense loyalty, his personal problem too. More and more, the lab technicians, doing a perfectly adequate job, felt the lash of Mark's tongue for some real or imagined infraction. And he began to perform what could only describe as alchemy - retaining small mysterious samples of special liquids which he insisted held the key to all the plant problems, once they could be sorted out. So Stan reluctantly replaced Mark with Leo as laboratory supervisor. From the point of laboratory operations, the move was an unqualified success. Personnel complaints ceased entirely as a Cape Breton supervisor began to work with Cape Breton technicians. Laboratory accuracy and speed did not suffer to any extent that Stan could determine.

Mark, of course, was crushed. Despite Stan's protestations, he felt that he had failed. As part of Stan's expanded effort to find anybody who could help with the plant technical problems, the Nova Scotia Research Foundation, in Halifax, had begun to work with CGE and Mark was appointed as their interface. Stan knew, because of Mark's communication challenges, the relationship was likely to be less than optimal. But they had good laboratory facilities, in which Mark could, Stan hoped, dabble endlessly. The appointment meant that Mark would transfer to NSRF in Halifax.

Soon after, the new operations manager, Reg Heasman, arrived. He was short, dapper, always immaculately dressed, and supremely self-confident. He looked somewhat like the English screen comedian, Dudley Moore. He had a nice sense of humor, and Stan had no qualms in turning over operations to him. At a short meeting with Lee, it was agreed that Stan's team would continue to specify the crucial parameters affecting extraction, namely GS process pressure, gas and liquid flows, and temperatures in all the towers. Everything else, including emergency operations, was Reg's job. Reg did insist, quite reasonably, that Stan's personnel must not touch controls, and process parameters would be provided in writing.

Now Stan was free to tackle the real problem, "Why did the plant misbehave, and why did it misbehave worse in winter? Everybody talked about foaming. Just what is foam, and what causes it? Why does beer foam and seven-up doesn't?" His head was buzzing with questions, too few of which had any answers. His foaming task force members were selected with care, only three people, because Stan didn't have the slightest idea what they would be doing. He chose Shin-der, for his superb analytical knowledge of how the process worked; Gordon, for his expertise in water chemistry; and Peter Chau, a young Chinese engineer.

Soon after that, Dave Lillie, the CR&D liaison engineer assigned to manage the Schenectady effort, came up to visit the plant. He was accompanied by Vic, who insisted he knew what caused the problem and how it could be fixed. He gave Stan's team a lecture on what caused foaming at the Dupont plant. From his point of view, it was all cut and dried. As water poured over the outlet weir of the top tray, it was of course frothing due to the gas entrapped in it. It then entered a downcomer on its way to the tray below. In the downcomer, since there was no gas being forced through the water, the froth was supposed to dissipate, leaving only water. However, as a safety margin, the downcomer was designed to work OK even if the water in the downcomer was a 70% gas/30% water mixture. If there was less than 30% water in the downcomer, it could not pass down all the water entering it, and the tray would 'flood' as more water entered it than could be taken away. Then the excess water would be carried away upwards by the gas stream. Although none of this could be seen in the GS process, it was, in general, a known phenomenon in separation technology, and it could be confirmed in the GS process by detecting the passage of the extra water through the compressor. The only solution when this happened was to cut the amount of water entering the tray. So far so good, and everyone nodded in agreement. If foam with too much gas in it persisted in the downcomer, the process could not work.

The million dollar question was, "What caused the foam?"

"Ah," said Vic, waving his hands expressively, "It's the aluminum carried over from the clarifier. You see, sometimes the water treatment operators add more aluminum sulphate than the clarifier needs. Then it's carried over in solution, enters the GS process, and causes the foaming."

Stan's team was still mystified, "How did it cause the foaming?"

Vic didn't know exactly, but he did know that any time the DuPont plant experienced foaming, the water treatment operators were adding more aluminum.

Stan's team checked this theory out, and at Savanah River, it did seem to hold water, excuse the pun, up to a point. The point being that foaming only occurred when the water treatment operators added more aluminum. The point not mentioned by Vic, was that sometimes extra aluminum was added and no foaming occurred. And there was no correlation between the Port Hawkesbury extraction problem and the amount of alum added to the clarifier. Nevertheless, the myth persisted at upper management levels. There was a period that year, as it became increasingly evident that a foaming problem was severely limiting extraction, that Reg Richardson would call Stan from Toronto several times a month to find out how many parts per million of aluminum was being added to the clarifier. Poor Reg. He had been instrumental in persuading GE to invest the $50 million, now approaching $100 million, to build this plant. Now its miserable performance, in financial as well as political terms, was being laid on his shoulders, and although he had committed those millions of dollars, he could do nothing but worry about a minor process detail. But however much he badgered, Stan had him cornered.

"Reg," Stan would say, "We're running about 23 parts per million aluminum today. That's what the lab tests say we need for best water quality. And the aluminum and iron carryovers are both below half a part per million, just like they normally are and just as they should be. If you want me to cut that aluminum dose, I'll be happy to do so. But I can't vouch for what will happen."

Reg would grumble and recite Vic's theories, but he was too much of a good CGE manager to take performance responsibility away from the man on the spot.

With Dave Lillie's help, a 'getting to know each other' trip to Schenectady was arranged. Lee, Stan, and two members of his task force went down to tell them how the plant worked and what they knew about why it didn't, which wasn't much. Very few trips 'back East' were routine. This particular spring day, the group made it from Halifax to Toronto, only to find the connection to Schenectady cancelled because of thunderstorms. Unperturbed, Lee told them to wait. Soon he came back and announced he had chartered a plane, and shortly thereafter the little team was ensconced in a comfortable six seater.

"Err, what about the thunderstorms?" asked a round-eyed Gordon, as Lee began to explore the bar.

"No problem," replied Lee cheerfully, "I've used these guys before. They've got weather radar. I've asked them to leave the cabin curtain open so we can watch." And watch we did, as the pilots picked there way round the numerous thunderstorms blocking the path to the Tri Cities airport. With lightning flickering all around, St Elmo's fire streaming from the wing tips, securely strapped in against the severe turbulence, and his own bar within reach, Lee seemed to thoroughly enjoy the flight. Stan noticed Gordon was not drinking and wondered if his stomach was as queasy as his own.

The next morning, the Port Hawkesbury contingent pitched their story to about 50 engineers and scientists, who, that afternoon, reciprocated with technology which they thought, might contribute to the problem. There was one pitch by their surface chemist, George Gaines, who considerably intrigued Stan, since for the first time he helped Stan understand the crucial physics of foams. It seems there are two basic kinds of molecules, called 'hydrophobic', from the Greek 'water fearing' and 'hydrophilic', from the Greek 'water loving'. The first kind, like gasoline and oil, are insoluble in water, while the second kind, like caustic soda and sugar, are soluble. If you can combine both properties in one molecule, you get a 'surface active molecule', abbreviated to 'surfactant', which tends to concentrate at the surface of the liquid, and causes water to foam by reducing its surface tension. The most well-known example is soap, which is made by combining a water insoluble animal fat with caustic soda. But surface active molecules also exist naturally, as can be seen in the little pools of froth which form in woodland streams.

"So, might there be surface active molecules in our raw water?" Stan asked George. "But, why do we foam in the plant some times and not others?"

"Beats me," replied George, "perhaps your clarifier doesn't always extract the surface active molecule." Shades of Vic, Stan thought. Perhaps he was right all the time. The two teams parted with many new ideas on both sides, and Dave promised to visit the plant soon with his plan for Schenectady actions.

No sooner had Lee taken over, than he was being badgered by CGE's customer, Atomic Energy of Canada Ltd. (AECL). They, of course, had an intense interest in the plant performance, since the entire Canadian nuclear power program was dependent on a plentiful supply of heavy water. AECL was marketing Canadian nuclear power technology around the world, in fierce competition with the USA giants, GE and Westinghouse. They could hardly sell any more Canadian nuclear power plants while a 500 MWe power plant was sitting idle in Ontario for lack of heavy water. By now it was common knowledge that the first heavy water plant AECL had contracted out at Glace Bay, about 80 miles north of Port Hawkesbury, was not working, and would probably never work as designed. An extensive rebuild would be required, taking time and money. Money AECL could pry out of the federal government, but time was not so easily obtained. AECL wanted to come into the Port

Hawkesbury plant to help solve our problems, through some unspecified miracle. Lee absolutely refused to have them on site, but did agree that we would work with them on our problem, sharing openly all our own, and Schenectady's, data and experimental results. So now, Stan had four interfaces to juggle: one with Reg for day to day extraction conditions, one with Schenectady, one with Nova Scotia Research foundation, and one with Chalk River, the research and development arm of AECL.

As if this were not enough, soon after the Foaming Task Force was constituted, a new personality appeared on the scene. CGE's parent company, GE, appointed a vice-president with complete authority to take any actions necessary regarding our operation. There was, at that time, a schizophrenic relationship between GE and CGE which probably persists to this day. Because of intense Canadian nationalism, CGE is a public company on the Toronto stock exchange. Its stock is traded like any other public company. However, within GE, CGE is treated just like any other operating division, with its own GE profit and loss reporting, and its strategic and financial plans fully controlled by the parent company. How could that be, you may ask, if CGE is a Canadian public company? Simple! Over 90% percent of the stock is held by GE! At this time, the financial performance of CGE was being hurt by the big investment and subsequent operating loss of the Port Hawkesbury plant, and that was never tolerated for long in any GE division.

The new vice-president was Roy Beaton. The plant was, in fact, very lucky with all of its American Big Brothers: first Reg, then Vic, then Dave, and now Roy. All these individuals had lots of ingenuity, technological ability, and competent management skills. They were wonderful people to be with, erudite, widely-read in both their own fields and public affairs, and able to explain to Stan many of the mysteries of both corporate and American politics. Roy was 6 feet tall, built like a running back, and trying hard to prevent the inevitable downhill slope of aging by a stern jogging routine. Much to the amazement of the locals, Roy maintained this routine every time he came to Port Hawkesbury, despite rain, shine, fog, snow or ice. If the weather was bad, Roy could be seen jogging under the covered walkway around the Port Hawkesbury shopping center, between about 6:00 and 6:30 am. Stan respectfully declined his offer to jog with him, preferring to meet him at the plant. Roy had handled the GE portion of the American man-on-the-moon program, which was close to a 10,000 person effort at its peak, and was therefore unfazed by demanding technology. He was between assignments when he began to work with CGE. Since he was operating out of Syracuse, New York, he had persuaded his own boss that he could use the GE corporate jet for his necessary travel to Canada. That was OK by Stan, since Roy would frequently arrange his travel to coincide with his own.

There was, for instance, a memorable joint trip to Chalk River. It was one of the first meetings of the 'Chemistry Working Party' which Stan had established jointly with AECL. He was somewhat puzzled as to why Lee and Roy would want to come along, since it was quite a low level 'technology only' meeting. But Lee said they wanted to show the customer that GE and CGE had top level management interest in solving the plant problems, an explanation Stan accepted at the time. Only much later did he find out there might have been another motivation. It was agreed that Lee and Stan would fly to Montreal, meet Roy, Dave and George in the corporate jet, and the whole group would fly up to Chalk River, about 200 miles to the west.

Stan went home that night with his head buzzing. "Listen, Joy. How about a few days' vacation in Montreal and Toronto? You could fly with me to Montreal, find something to do there for a couple of days, and then meet me at that station just by the airport. I've always wanted to take that train trip along the St Lawrence to Toronto." So a few days later he said goodbye to her in the Montreal airport with a firm caution, "Now look. That 5:15 pm train to Toronto is the last and we've got to be on it. I know what you are like when you get to those Montreal shops. Make sure you're at the station by 5 pm at the latest."

"But how can you be sure you'll be there?" she questioned.

"Roy has told me that he positively has to be back early tomorrow night, and has said we'll definitely leave Chalk River before 4 pm. Don't worry about me. I'll be there."

Lee and Stan met the Schenectady team on the commuter side of the airport, and the compact 12 seat Caravelle jet took off through thick clouds. About 45 minutes later the pilot came back to talk to us, leaving his co-pilot at the controls. "I think I'm there," he said, "But I can't raise anyone on the radio. I'm going down to have a look."

After what seemed an interminable descent, we broke out of the clouds, perhaps 2000 feet above the ground, over what looked like featureless fields. We began to circle. The pilot came back again, "There's a grass strip down there with a car waiting. Is that it?" he asked. Everybody agreed it probably was.

After landing, the lone driver provided by AECL was apologetic, "I was told there would only be four. I'm afraid I can't fit seven in this car."

"No problem" replied Roy. "Where's the nearest rental car location."

The driver shifted his feet uncomfortably, "I'm afraid that's at Chalk River."

"OK. One of us will pick up a car and come back and get the others," suggested Roy.

The driver looked even more uncomfortable. "It's about a one hour drive to Chalk River. By the time you got there, rent a car, got back here and back to Chalk River, half of the day would be gone. I was told to deliver you for lunch."

Roy was determined, "Then what about a taxi?"

The driver brightened. "Yeah, I think there is a guy near here who does taxi's. Let me give him a call." And so we finally arrived at Chalk River, and business began. George, being the only one with spare cash, got stuck with the taxi bill. That night, AECL provided accommodation and meals at their hostel, a first class facility used both by new employees and visiting scientists and assorted big-wigs.

The following day, about lunch time, the pilots conferred with

Roy. They explained, "We've phoned for weather briefings, and it's not looking good. If you really want to make Syracuse by 6 tonight, we'll get out to the field early, and have everything warmed up. Be sure you're there no later than 4." Roy agreed. The pilots, having no cash, told the taxi to return to pick up George and Dave. The expense account for that trip, so George said later, raised some eyebrows at Schenectady. It showed $6.00 for meals and accommodation, and $325.00 for taxis! The party re-assembled at the field about 4 pm and to Stan's relief, they were soon airborne. He relaxed as Lee opened the bar.

"No problem now in meeting Joy at the station," Stan thought to himself. "I wonder if we can get a real dinner on the train, or just one of those cardboard snacks?" Shortly, they broke through the overcast clouds and the pilot came back again.

"Montreal's socked in," he announced cheerfully, "I'll drop you Canadian guys off in Toronto."

Stan's mind began to whirl. "Err, what time do you expect to land?" he asked.

"Oh, about 5 o'clock, give or take a few minutes. Depends on how congested the commuter side is and how soon they clear us in for landing." Stan fidgeted and fussed until they landed and he was first out of the door into the little general aviation terminal. After a tussle with enquiries, he got through to the station in Montreal. It was now about 5:05 pm. An unmistakable Quebec accent answered in French, and he fought down his consternation.

"Do you speak English?" Stan asked.

"But of course," was the reply.

"This is an emergency," continued Stan, "My wife is waiting at the station and I must speak to her at once. Can you page Mrs. Davies?"

" "ow do you spell zat?" requested the guy. Swearing under his breath, he spelt it out. Over the phone, he could hear a train rumbling into the station as the page was announced.

Finally, Joy's voice came over the phone. "Where are you? What's going on?" she asked.

"I'm in Toronto. Can you still make that train?"

"What are you doing in Toronto? How did you get there?"

"Never mind that, can you make that train?"

"I don't know. It's 5:13 and I've got to cross the tracks. Why didn't you meet me here, as you said you would?"

Stan's patience broke. "Never mind that," he raved, "Catch the damn train and I'll meet you here."

"You've got some explaining to do!" she said frostily, and rang off.

So, Stan stood up his wife in Montreal and never got to enjoy his train ride along the St Lawrence River.

The plant began to show its characteristic improvement as spring wore on, and extraction had improved to 75% of the design value as the summer shutdown started. There were a number of essential things to do, and the GS process was pumped clear of H_2S, for both safety and convenience. Maintenance was so much easier when there was no gas to worry about. Much to everyone's relief, the tower trays were in fine condition, clean and undamaged. At least the plant personnel had learned to produce without ruining the equipment.

There were three key experiments which were being installed at the request of the foaming task force. Stan's team really wanted to measure the pressure drop across the top cold tower tray. That should show conclusively when foaming was starting. Unfortunately, there was no way to do it, short of drilling holes in the towers, which was vetoed on safety grounds. However, it was possible to get a measurement across the top half of the cold tower, 26 trays in all, which turned out to be almost as useful. Secondly, an 'isokinetic probe' was inserted in the compressor suction pipe. This grand sounding device was merely to sample water drawn into the compressor suction from the top tray. The theory was that this should sample the foam.

Finally, Stan's team had their most important windfall. The Union Carbide Company, who had designed and manufactured the sieve trays, was of course intensely interested in their performance. They offered to install a window to see the tray operating. Who would have thought that a window was an option? You are probably saying, "You've spent the last hundred pages saying how dangerous this process is, and you're going to put a window into a vessel with 300 psi H_2S?"

Union Carbide had been very ingenious. Their window, which fitted a manhole cover, was a stainless steel disc with two four inch diameter portholes. Each port had a thick disc of Perspex, held in by compression rings. "We've tested it to 500 psi," they said, "And it doesn't leak. We'll lend it to you for nothing if you'll put it where we can see a cold tray operating."

Stan dug out his old safety calculations, and showed a leak would not be fatal off-site, even if the Perspex blew out completely, since the window was 250 feet above the ground. The only risk, if it did develop a leak, was that the tower would have to be shut down and emptied of H_2S, to repair it. It speaks volumes for the interest in how the trays operated that Stan was able to get approval for this experiment so easily, since Lee, Ted, and Reg were not about to cut any corners where safety was concerned. It was installed in the GS process for at least three years, and never caused any trouble.

As this shutdown was drawing to a close, Dave Lillie advised Stan that the manager of Corporate Research and Development wanted to come up to see the plant, and hear what progress had been made. "We haven't made any progress yet," Stan objected. "This isn't a laboratory where you can cobble something together in a few weeks. This is a production plant. And none of these experiments we've put in will generate any useful data 'til Christmas."

Dave calmed him down. "Relax, Stan. Remember, Art is putting a lot of his money into this, none of which was budgeted last year. He just wants to see where it's going." After a tour of the plant, Dave and Stan found themselves presenting their planned work to four, yes four, corporate vice-presidents. There was Reg Richardson, the VP from CGE head office, his boss from GE, Roy, and the VP from corporate research and development, as well as Art Beucher, who had initially asked for the review. Apart from Reg, who flew in the day before, the other three had come by corporate jet that morning to Halifax, drove for three hours, and arrived about 10 am. Stan shuddered to think what time they got up. After coffee, a plant tour, and a catered lunch, the visitors seemed decidedly somnolent. As Dave and Stan launched into their dog and pony show, eyes began to droop and close. Art, in particular, seemed to dose through most of the pitch, and the few questions from others were easy to field. Stan went first, and began to relax as Dave drew to a close. This had been easier than he thought. Then Art asked permission to speak, and launched into a devastating critique of the plan. His comments showed he had heard and understood, sometimes better than the speakers, every word uttered. Without once raising his voice, or in any way being discourteous, he made Stan and Dave feel like undergraduates in a college seminar. He approved of all the things planned, but listed half a dozen more to be tried. Since most of them were aimed at Schenectady's half of the plan, Stan was again able to breathe easier.

Afterwards Dave was philosophical. "Well, that's Art for you. He's really a brilliant guy. I guess nobody can doubt GE's intention to sort out this problem. At least he can't grumble when I go back and ask for more money."

After this exposure to Art, Stan began to appreciate why GE's Corporate Research and Development Center had made such a name for itself. With that quality of management, they could trounce the world, but could they solve the foaming problem?

8 THE WASHING MACHINE

In late summer, the plant restarted and quickly resumed extraction at about 75%. Reg was all for raising pressure and flow immediately to 100%, but, with two disastrous winters behind him, Stan was cautious. He did allow the pressure to go up to about 280 psi, and throughput was slowly raised to over 80%. The window into C tower was a wonder, especially once a light was shone in through one port, so that the inside of the tower could be seen in the other port. But what was seen was decidedly uninteresting. There was the top tray froth, running across the tray, over the weir, and down the downcomer, just like it was supposed to do, and just like it did in Union Carbide's laboratory. The window was about three feet above the tray, and you could get quite a good view looking down on it. The froth height marker, like a miniature TV antenna, stood upright, blackening but unbowed, indicating about a 10 inch froth height. There was one thing nobody expected. A thin fog filled the space above the tray, the droplets of water glistening in the light, and moving upwards with the gas flow. Finally, gravity was overcome, Stan thought to himself.

In the summer shutdown, there had only been time to install the 'tie-ins' for our other two experiments, that is, the connections to the tower which could not readily be made while the process was operating. Neither of these two experiments was yet working when, a few weeks after start up, the Union Carbide engineers visited Port Hawkesbury to see one of their sieve trays operating under pressure in H_2S.

"There's really nothing to see," Stan told them as they buckled on their escape bottles. "Just like in the lab, although the froth height is a bit higher than you and Shin-Der expected. It's quite stable and so is the GS process since we started up. Reg wants me to authorize another flow increase."

The Union Carbide engineers left the elevator at the top platform, walked past the spidery thin third stage towers, and started the ascent to the top walkway by C tower. Stan let his visitors go on ahead as he stopped to inspect the progress on piping up the top tray 'delta P'. "If they don't get this job completed before winter sets in, nobody will be able to work up here." he thought.

His musings were interrupted by a call from his companions. "Hey, Stan, I thought you said the froth height was normal. Look at this." Hurrying up the last few steps, Stan came face to face with a $100 million, once in a lifetime, spectacle. Foam was churning across the middle of the view port. Like a giant washing machine, thick brown soapy suds lapped at the window. The froth height marker was completely buried under what must have been three feet of foaming liquid. As he watched, mesmerized, the line of froth moved slowly upwards until it completely covered the window. Only soapy bubbles could now be seen.

"Holy cow," Stan said stupidly in unbelief, "It's foaming."

His companions brought him back to his senses. "What do they say in the control room? Is it unstable? Can they see anything?"

Stan raced to the elevator, and fumed as it slowly rose to the top platform. Inside, he called the shift supervisor from the telephone. "What's going on down there? Is C tower OK? Any sign of instability?"

"Everything's fine here," came Gerard's voice, "Hang on while I check the panel." And then after a pause, "Everything's fine. Steady as a rock."

"Well it won't be for long," Stan replied. "You've got over four feet of foam at the top of C tower, and you'd better get ready to cut the flow. I'm on my way down."

Now everybody knew: unequivocally, absolutely, no ifs, ands or buts. The process foamed. And there was more. Our old, old experiment, with the little H_2S tower, done before the plant was built, and which purported to show no foaming, was wrong. Not only wrong, but misleading. And there was still more. None of the instruments which the operators had available to them could warn them that foaming was beginning. Stan shuddered to remember that first winter of operation, when the flow was increased, slowly, they thought. Foam must have piled up on the top of the tower until great gobs of it were sucked down the huge gas pipe, through the compressor and sprayed into the bottom of the hot tower. No wonder those bottom trays in the hot towers were ruined, swept away as if a fire hose was sprayed on a wooden fence. It was a wonder the compressors survived.

The elevator really got a workout that morning as everyone, even those not fond of heights, had to go to see the marvelous foaming tower. Of course, soon after the flow was cut, the foam decreased and then disappeared; only a few people were lucky enough to see the foam surface slowly subside back across the window. By afternoon, the tray looked normal, behaving as though butter wouldn't melt in its mouth. A few days thereafter, under Stan's urgent pleading, the second experimental instrument, measuring the pressure drop across the top 26 trays, was put into service. The Foaming Task Force conducted its first, very first, planned experiment; the antifoam additive, mixed with the feedwater, was stopped. A pair of operators, with a radio, stationed by C tower window supplemented Stan's anxious team in the control room. Soon the expected call came in; "The foam is beginning to rise." The tray 'delta P' indication in the control room began to rise in concert. The antifoam was restored, and, just as gradually as it started, the foam, and the 'delta P' reading subsided. Stan heaved a sigh of relief. At least the operators now had a device which warned them of approaching instability, and allowed them to cut flow before things got out of hand. His Foaming Task Force had achieved its first real success.

The autumn had been fairly mild by Cape Breton standards, and the locals were hopeful for an 'open' winter, with lots of rain and little ice. But in mid-December, there was a precipitous drop in temperature, accompanied soon after by a howling north-westerly. The wind whipped waves on Landrie Lake and prevented ice formation, but cooled the surface so rapidly that violent convection currents roiled the waters. This caused a very rare phenomena, the legendary 'frazil ice'. Notwithstanding that ice always forms on the surface of water, Cape Breton and Landrie Lake were out to demonstrate otherwise. The lake cooling was so rapid, and the turbulence so great, that water at the freezing point was carried below the surface, where tiny needlelike ice crystals formed. These were swept onto the intake screens of the pumphouse, and soon began to obstruct the flow of water.

As the morning shift came on duty December 8th, it was to face a total loss of water. A shutdown was inevitable. After the howling wind dropped, the lake froze almost instantly on the surface and simultaneously the intake screen ice melted. The plant was restarted immediately, since this was no weather to be shut down. But unbeknownst to Stan's engineers, the water quality had changed dramatically virtually overnight. The GS process ceased to extract at the same conditions where it had worked perfectly just a day before.

Stan's engineers were confused, for a time, because the sample lines, used to draw water samples from the towers, froze, (hydrated, really) and control became difficult. But the effluent samples showed extraction had fallen almost to zero. Once more the miserable process of cutting the gas and water flows went on until the compressors again screamed their complaint. There was no choice but reduce the pressure and flows until the GS process started to work again. By January 1973, water throughput was back to about 60% once more. As the winter wore on, at least the process was stable. The tussles with the stripper level got fewer and fewer as the operators learned to use their new foaming indicator. Reg Heasman got more and more unhappy, impatient and disgruntled, as he watched the GS extraction steadily decline.

The guys from Schenectady and Stan's team caucused to review what they had learned. It turned out to be not much. "When not foaming, the tray is operating normally," reported Shin-Der. "The froth height is slightly higher than expected from laboratory measurements in air, about 10% perhaps." They had agreed to use the word 'froth' when the tray was operating normally and 'foam' when it wasn't. The crucial difference was that froth was sustained by gas bubbling through the water, whereas foam could persist in the absence of a gas flow.

"The clarifier is operating about the same in winter as in summer." stated Gordon. "There is no change in water quality that we can see. Aluminum, iron, and organics are all about the same. Perhaps the floc is a bit smaller and lighter in the winter, but that could be just the temperature."

"Our Lab hasn't turned up anything yet." reported Dave Lillie. "The trouble is, we can't duplicate your conditions."

"But, it's got to be something in the water." Stan complained. "Why can't you analyze what organic compounds are present?"

"Your treated water is really pretty good," replied George, "and it's only got a few parts per million of organic compounds in it. In the small quantities I can take back with me, we can't identify what they are."

So began the legend of the 'border troll', who lived in an unknown cave somewhere between the USA and Canada, and constantly thwarted efforts to ship material from one site to the other. On one occasion, George actually located the troll's temporary cave, a shipping trailer shunted onto a remote part of the Halifax airport. Apparently, this cave is a home for forgotten and unloved materials without paperwork. Sure enough, urgently needed GE equipment was in that particular trailer.

Attempts to get substantial quantities of Port Hawkesbury water back to Schenectady, in particular, constantly backfired. George began to take back a liter or two at a time. Soon the inevitable happened. "Are you bringing anything back into the USA?" the border customs agent asked George.

"Only a few industrial samples." was George's standard reply, which usually sufficed. Not this time.

"Open this bag please." The agent ruffled through the assortment of dirty clothes, plastic bags, and bottles. Brushing aside small plastic bags of a white powder, looking suspiciously like cocaine, but actually a selection of our water treatment chemicals, the agent seized on one of the liter plastic bottles filled with water.

"What's this?" he growled suspiciously.

"Just water." replied George bravely.

"Why would anybody bring back water to the USA?" the agent wanted to know. George began to explain, but the agent cut him short.

"How can I tell it's only water?" he asked.

"Look, it's printed on the label." replied George. There in large handwritten letters, (George's handwriting, if the truth be known) it stated: "Port Hawkesbury Feedwater, 12/7/72" This explanation seemed to satisfy customs and George was allowed to proceed.

"We can't go on like this." complained George at the next meeting. "Those damn bottles leak when I take them up to altitude in the plane. My wife wants to know why my dirty underwear is always damp when I get back from Port Hawkesbury. We need tens of gallons, not just a liter or two." So a large collapsible plastic container was dully acquired, filled with water, and turned over to the shipping department. They had a wooden crate made to fit, and shipped the box to Schenectady, COD.

George called Stan up a couple of weeks later. "You know that ten gallons of water you shipped us?"

"Yeah, of course. Has it arrived?" asked Stan.

"Well, yes and no. When your carpenters packed it, one of the nails went right through the wood and into the plastic container. It arrived empty. Can you do it again?"

Stan swore and turned the problem over to Peter Chau, "...And Peter, make sure you personally watch every step of that packing until the damn thing leaves our site."

Now the strain was beginning to tell. There never seemed to be enough time. The numbers and the data, the trips and the trip reports, the chemistry and the analysis, the plant performance and process conditions, were overwhelming. Stan's mind seemed so full of technicalities that there was no room for his wife and family.

Finally, one trip brought him to his senses. Lee and Stan drove to Halifax and flew to Toronto. Lee did his business with Reg, while Stan flew up to Chalk River and back. When they met at the airport for the return flight, Halifax was fogged in, but Air Canada would fly them to Saint John and bus them from there. Trying to write his trip report on the plane, Stan's mind refused to function. He got up to go to the toilet. Leaning his head on the bulkhead wall, he unzipped his pants and waited for the urine stream to flow. The engine of the DC9 thrummed, only a foot or two from him. Idly, he began to wonder, "What was the chance of a blade detaching from that engine and slicing through the limp piece of flesh he held in his hand. Let's see, perhaps 20,000 rpm, the rotor couldn't be more than a foot in diameter at the root. The radius times the square of the angular velocity divided by 32…that would be about 10,000 g's. In stress, that would be… And then he stopped. Surely all these numbers and facts were irrelevant. What was he doing with his life? Why were numbers paramount? Didn't people matter anymore? Was his brain just a computer? And if so, who switched it on and off? And why didn't he or she write better programs?" Back at his seat, he dozed fitfully until the DC9 landed at Saint John, sliding sideways to a stop at the end of the icy runway.

By the time they were bused to Halifax, picked up their car, and started on their return to Port Hawkesbury, even Lee called uncle. "I'm not going to fight this fog and ice all night." he growled. "Let's pull off in Truro and grab a room for the night." It was 1:00 am before Stan put his head on the pillow, so weary that the sounds of partying, apparently coming from a nearby room, or perhaps the corridor, did not keep him awake. He vaguely heard a banging on an adjacent door, and raucous laughter. But at 2:30 am he came wide awake. The hotel was quiet except for a low moaning coming from the adjacent room. "Oh, no... no no." a woman was gasping. He sat bolt upright, sweating. Was she being murdered? He leapt out of bed and put his ear to the partition wall. Then, on hearing the mattress creaking, enlightenment, relief, and silent laughter, swept over him. A honeymoon! Twice more that night he was aroused by the same moaning, but awoke refreshed.

Stan met Lee for breakfast in a great mood. "Let's sit where we can see the door." he said gaily, "I want to watch who comes in." Lee looked at him shrewdly.

"Well, you must have had a good night," he observed, "I was getting worried about you yesterday. You seemed rather down." Stan told him what had raised his spirits. Stan never did see the honeymoon couple, but at least Joy seemed pleased with his ministrations that night.

Not all trips finished so pleasantly. A few weeks later, Stan returned one morning to find Rex had died, suddenly, unexpectedly and tragically. Shoveling snow, he had a heart attack, and collapsed in a chair in front of his wife. This was the first death the plant had experienced, and there was no protocol to deal with it. Rex had not been a popular figure on the plant. Although always civil and friendly to management, he had succeeded in alienating several of the operations staff with whom he worked more directly. Nonetheless, all rallied round to give what comfort there was to be given to his wife, Beverly. She was a diminutive woman, always in Rex's shadow, and seemingly subservient to his wishes and desires. But, she had brought up five fine children. That night several people gathered at her house to offer what comfort they could. Nobody knew what to say, and the evening was mostly spent in dismal trivia.

Later, a full blown Roman Catholic Cape Breton funeral occurred. Not a religious man, to Stan the service seemed lamentable, the priest trying to wring the last ounce of grief from the silent, shivering, weeping, little figure in black. Outside, it began to snow, the flakes moving horizontally with the coffin as the pall bearers carried it to the grave. Then there was more of the same, until poor Beverly, weighed down with the tragedy of it all and sobbing piteously, had to be supported by her sons. At last it was over, and the participants and pall bearers went back to work. As troubled as the plant may be, at least it represented life, progress, the hope for a better future, something to be influenced by man's efforts.

To make matters worse, a few weeks later, Stan got a call from the Nova Scotia Research Foundation in Halifax. Mark had not shown up for work one day. After repeated calls to his apartment, the police had been sent, only to find him dead on his couch. The cause of death was never determined. Stan shed a few tears.

Although sometimes a pain, Mark had been a hard working colleague and a loyal and devoted friend. Stan's mind went back to when Bill, the finance manager, came to him. "Hey, Stan, you've got a problem. Mark has been coming in to work at night and telephoning someone in Sydney."

"Well, we've got suppliers and consultants all over the continent. So what?" Stan replied.

"These bills are hundreds of dollars per month, to one private house," Bill explained.

So Stan had called Mark in and had it out with him. It turned out to be a new girlfriend. Mark hung his head, "Oh. Mr. Davies. Even Mark can be a fool and fall in love." And now he was gone.

The winter dragged on, and morale began to droop. The foaming task force came up with no more breakthroughs. To be sure, the plant was stable, but at a low extraction rate. The cause of the foaming, and more importantly, a cure for it, seemed as far away as ever.

Despite the best efforts of the various laboratories, no obvious surfactant could be found in the water. As George said, "The trouble is I can't imagine a surfactant so potent that it could cause the heavy foams you see in that sight glass. To get those thick soapy suds, you need a high concentration of a surfactant. That's why you add a whole cup of Tide to your washing machine. To get real thick, stable, foam in nature, the surfactant is normally concentrated in some way."

Stan was intrigued. "Concentrated? How?"

"Well, think of the little foam pad floating in an eddy of a forest stream. It only forms because the surfactant, concentrated at the surface of the water, is constantly enriched by new water carried to it. Then the foam traps it, and it concentrates it. If you could actually measure the surfactant in the film of one of those bubbles, it would be hundreds or thousands of times more concentrated than in the water itself. That's presumably why we can't find it in the water samples you've sent us."

"You think that our process is concentrating the surfactant? How?" asked Stan. But George didn't know.

Reg Heasman began to get impatient. He pushed to raise the water flow, and Stan reluctantly conceded. After all, winter had set in, and things got better in the spring. Perhaps they already were. But, foaming began almost immediately.

"Nothing to show for it," Stan said wearily, "Cut the flow again."

The next day, one of the engineers working for Reg, sneaked into Stan's office saying, "Hey, Stan. Have you seen the process flow charts? Have you seen what that crazy guy is doing?"

"No. What's Reg doing? We've cut the flow, haven't we?"

"Cut the flow my ****. He's got the L/G so far out of whack the process couldn't extract even if it wasn't foaming." Appalled, Stan hurried into the control room. One glance at the control charts, lying in the shift supervisor's office, confirmed his informant's intelligence. The red and green dots, lined up at the bottom of the graph, showed extraction was zero. A glance at the control panel confirmed the liquid flow had been cut by almost 50%, while the gas flow was unchanged from yesterday. The first principal of the GS process, keeping the L/G at 0.52, had been violated.

Stan appealed to Reg in vain. "You've had your turn," Reg said, "for almost a year. Now I'm going to try."

"But the process can't possibly work as you've got it set. At least get the L/G back where it should be," Stan pleaded.

Reg was airily dismissive. "I don't believe all your theory crap. Haven't you heard of hill climbing theory? I'll discover the optimum production settings experimentally."

Stan crept back to his office, stunned, shaken and cowed. After all, in a way, Reg was right. He had his turn. For 18 months, not just the 12 months Reg had seen. And what had he accomplished? He had stabilized the plant at about 50% design production level, a level which could never be economic. Stan sank into his chair and swiveled to catch the glorious view. The frigid late winter wind ruffled the strait, and the setting sun glinted on the waves. Just what was he doing here? He was no chemical process engineer. What made him think he could solve a problem which had some of the best brains in the country stumped? After a few more minutes of soul searching, he marched in to see Lee.

"Lee, I don't think I can make any further contribution here," he said. "My foaming task force doesn't seem to be going anywhere. Will you see if you can find me another job somewhere in CGE. Perhaps back in their Nuclear Division, where I came from."

Lee sat back, shifted position slightly to pass wind, and regarded Stan quizzically, "Not so long ago you were full of Gordon's idea to reduce the organic with activated carbon. What's happened?"

Stan opened his mouth to reply, and then all the frustrations of the last two years poured over him. He swallowed to avoid the tears starting. Then, like a penitent son in the confessional, all his troubles came pouring out. "Look, Lee, I'm buzzing between Schenectady, Chalk River and Halifax like a blue assed fly. Nobody has the faintest idea of what's wrong. Gordon's activated carbon idea is the only one that makes any sense, and that's going to be dirty and expensive, with no guarantee it will work. And now Reg is taking over the process control. You don't need me."

Lee looked at him thoughtfully, and to give himself time to think, tore a corner of paper from his pad, and chewed it ruminatively. It was a standing joke that most of Lee's pads were never used for writing. He asked a few more questions and pondered awhile. "Will you give me a few days? Today is Thursday. I'll let you know next week."

Stan was emotionally drained. "Take all the time you need, Lee. Just get me out of here."

Now Lee had a real decision on his hands. Stan was obviously as technically sound on the process as anyone he had met; perhaps not as good as Vic, but broader in his knowledge base. On the other hand, he had been in this backward neck of the woods for a long time, and lately had started exhibiting many of the signs of burn out. The emotion underlying Stan's request for re-assignment was obvious, and clearly triggered by Reg's action. Was there anyone else he knew, on site or off, who had a better chance of finding out what was wrong? And within a reasonable time? What about Reg? Reg had come to him from an overseas division of Polymer, quite highly recommended. He was reputed to be competent in chemical operations, and with good management skills. Was the recommendation sound, or was it just to get a non-performer transferred? Lee, who had faced many such problems in his career, began to systematically think through his options, and to formulate a plan.

The following Monday, Lee's Audi was already in the parking lot when Stan got to work. For Lee to be at work, with his office door closed, before Stan arrived, was a rare event. Later Dave King stuck his head in Stan's office, "What's going on?"

"I don't know," Stan replied, "What do you mean, what's going on?"

"Reg has been closeted with Lee for over two hours. The Monday morning production planning meeting has been cancelled."

"I haven't the faintest idea." Stan said airily, but his heart sank. They were undoubtedly deciding how to organize the management team once he left.

Later, Stan happened to be in the large, open, engineering office as Lee's door opened and a bemused Reg came out, "I've been fired. I've got until midday to clear my office." were his last words to anyone.

Dave King was called into Lee's office next. He came out equally bemused. "I've been promoted to Operations Manager. Lee wants to see you, Stan."

Lee was blunt and refused to discuss what had happened between himself and Reg. "I want you to take the Process Engineering Managers job," he barked. "The laboratory and production control. Dave has agreed he'll take process production settings from you. Ted will stay as Maintenance Manager. Now what about that activated carbon trial you and Gordon were talking about? What equipment will we need? When are we going to get started? And another thing, if you don't think these off-site laboratories are helping you, ignore them! Get on with your own ideas!"

Stan was caught completely off guard. For the second time, his action had precipitated a totally unexpected event, and a second operations manager had bit the dust. "As God is my witness," he thought bemusedly, "that was the last outcome I expected. Once again, a Production Manager has been fired and I benefit." Stan could hardly deny Lee's request.

"You cunning old bastard," Stan thought, "you had it all planned. Get rid of Reg first, make sure there wouldn't be the same kind of problems between Dave and myself as there were with Reg, and then present me with a 'fait accompli', my old job back."

The old gang, Leo, the lab techs, and a smattering of process engineers and chemists came back into Stan's fold with every appearance of delight. Reg had apparently not been an easy guy to work for. Nobody understood his thinking, and to those used to Stan's systematic and thoughtful way of talking through problems, Reg's management style seemed capricious and mysterious. Lee's faith in Stan buoyed his spirits, but the plant was still at 50% design extraction. There was work to be done.

Activated carbon was known to have the ability to remove organics from water. In these pollution conscious days, a carbon filter to purify your water can be bought at any hardware store. In the 1970's, it was a known, but little used technique. The trouble was, and is, it works by surface absorption, not by volume absorption. Activated carbon is highly porous, filled with microscopic pores and channels, and the organic particles attach themselves to the large surface area so exposed. But when the surface is covered, it loses its effectiveness. Remember that, you folks who think that a carbon filter is the last word in health. You've got to replace it frequently. A carbon bed filter to remove organics from the enormous volume of water the plant used would be prohibitively expensive, and the carbon would either have to be replaced periodically, or reactivated by steam heating or roasting to drive off the accumulated organic material. Anyway you do it, it would be an expensive proposition with no certainty of any return in increased production. Gordon came up with the breakthrough.

"You know," he mused one day, "Our clarifier is already taking out about half the organics in the raw water. That means some organic material is attaching itself to the aluminum hydroxide floc. Suppose we added activated carbon to the clarifier? The carbon would attach to the floc and be removed from the water, taking the organics with it." Laboratory experiments confirmed his thoughts.

So, some tanks were fitted up, a large supply of activated carbon acquired, and temporary 'carbon trial operators' were hired, two for each shift. Their job was to mix the 50 lb. bags of activated carbon into a slurry in a small tank. Stan even made a solemn little training videotape, pouring beer and seven-up into glasses, to show what causes foam, and played it for all the personnel.

"You see," he said, pouring seven-up into a glass, "This liquid has gas trapped in it, but when the gas escapes, there's just a froth on top, which goes away as soon as the gas has finished bubbling out. But when we switch to beer, a good head of foam builds up as the gas escapes, and the foam persists for quite a long time, even after the gas has stopped bubbling out. That's because there are specific organics in the beer which lower the surface tension and stabilize the foam. We're going to add activated carbon to the clarifier. This will remove the bad acting organics, stop the foaming in the GS towers, and allow us to increase production."

Just before the trial began, his engineers confirmed nearness to the tower's foaming limit by stopping the anti-foam. Sure enough, the characteristic foam soon appeared. Then addition of the carbon began, and as soon as laboratory tests confirmed the water's organic content was indeed reduced, the antifoam was stopped again. Miracle of miracles, no foaming! Score two for the foaming task force! But it was a messy business. The activated carbon was in the form of a fine powder, supplied in sealed 50 lb. bags. It got everywhere as soon as a bag was opened. The building in which the carbon slurry was mixed soon took on the appearance of a coal mine. A few days after the trial began, a blackened Gordon dropped wearily into a chair in Stan's office and sighed wearily. "You know," he said, "we ought to hire women for this work, not men."

"What on earth for," Stan objected, "It's strenuous, messy work."

Gordon grinned wickedly. "Yeah, but at least when they went to the john, they wouldn't leave black fingerprints all over their personal anatomy."

The plant raw water treatment equipment was now producing 10,000 gallons per minute of the purest water imaginable. Measurements showed the 'TOC', total organic carbon, of the raw water to be about 5 parts per million. Prior to the carbon trial, the plant feedwater ran about 2.5 - 3.0 parts per million. Now it was 0.6 parts per million. The clarifier was now getting out almost 90% of Landrie Lake's organic poison.

Even the Schenectady team was impressed. They had recently devised a Rube Goldberg device for measuring the relative foaming propensity of different liquids. It was a small stainless steel cylinder, which could be filled with water and H_2S at up to 300 psi, and which had a small microphone attached to it. The cylinder was mounted on the end of a bar which could be shaken in a controlled manner. Then, by listening to the sounds made by the sloshing mixture, they could tell if it was foaming or not. Or so they claimed. It was, of course, of absolutely no use to the plant, although they insisted on shipping a copy of the contraption to Port Hawkesbury in case a use could be found for it, which it never was.

George called one day. "Stan, you remember I brought some of your latest, best, carbon treated water back with me? Well, I gave it to our foam test people, and asked them how it compared with Schenectady water. They used our distilled water, then double distilled water, and finally our best, ultra-pure, triple distilled water. They say your stuff is better than anything we've got down here." So in this backward part of Cape Breton, where only one radio station playing interminable country and western music could be heard, where if you didn't like hockey on a Saturday night you might as well go to bed since both TV channels carried it, where people took a drive on Sunday mornings after church to see the latest car smash, where not one person in a hundred could spell deuterium, here, here was the purest water in the world, 10,000 gallons of it every minute, crafted from a mixture of rain run-off, wood sludge and deer piss. Stan was pretty proud of what had been accomplished.

Even though the GS process was now fairly stable, the plant could still provide a surprise. One day, the entire control panel, including the indicator lights on the electrical distribution panel, went dark. Every level, pressure and flow indicator fell to zero. Even the lights went out, and an eerie silence pervaded the control room. "Jesus" grumbled Joe, the disconsolate control room operator, "Another power failure. And this one looks like a doozy."

Joe tried to raise the field operators on the control room radio, which was, of course, dead. He borrowed Gerry's portable radio and called his No 1 field operator. "OK, John, let's start the procedure for power failure shutdown. Close AM-610."

There was a moment of silence, and then John replied, "What do you mean, power failure shutdown? Everything's running fine down here. I'm by B tower compressor. Listen…" Over the radio came the healthy roar of a compressor.

Dave was in the control room at the time and he stared at Gerry in horror. All the plant equipment was running as though nothing had happened, but the operators were absolutely blind and helpless in the control room. Worse, most of the levels in the towers, including the all-important stripper, were controlled by automatic valves which constantly adjusted the flow to keep a constant level. With the loss of all automatic signals, these control valves 'froze' in their current position. The tower levels would, therefore, be increasing or decreasing, at random. And the operator had no knowledge of where the levels really were. There was real danger if the stripper level went low, since H_2S could be blown out to the effluent ditch. And a flooded tower could seriously damage the trays.

Dave got it first, "The non-interruptible power!" he gasped, and they both raced down stairs and burst into the little room which housed the non-interruptible power system. It was a little AC/DC generator, normally powered from the mains, but powered by a pair of large batteries if the external power failed. Then the generator ran off these batteries, as long as they lasted. All the instruments, and certain other selected equipment, ran on the power from this DC generator. If the mains failed, the DC power would continue uninterrupted for about 15 minutes. The room was occupied by one small inoffensive janitor, who was industriously sweeping the floor with his back to the small electrical control panel. He gaped at the intruders in wonder.

"Mother of God," whispered Dave. "Look. He's knocked off the main disconnect with his broom handle. That's why all the instrument power has gone. Now what do we do?" He answered his own question almost as soon as he asked it. "We've got to reconnect this power sooner or later. The longer we wait, the worse the situation gets. If we have to shut her down, at least we'll know what's happening. Gerry, go back upstairs, and tell Joe that the power is coming back."

Gerry shot back upstairs as Dave grasped the disconnect and firmly rotated it. There was a slight moan from the generator as it took up the load. Upstairs the lights came on and instruments resumed their indications. Joe and Gerry hovered by the purge and stripper panel, their eyes flicking over the alarms and readings. The transient was actually quite minor, since control had only been lost for about two or three minutes, and the plant stayed on line with only little jiggles on the strip chart recorders to show anything had been amiss. Dave insisted on a padlock on the non-interruptible power room door, and gave the key to the shift supervisor.

As Stan rejoiced in the success of the carbon trial, and instructed his engineers to begin a careful, measured, increase in flow rates, a defining moment in his life occurred. He was working late, pacing up and down in the control room like Captain Hornblower on the deck of his flagship, no doubt irritating the control room operator hugely. He was thinking of foaming caused by concentrated organic surfactant, when suddenly his mind flashed to those little drops of mist, moving upwards in the tower, against gravity, and against the normal downward flow of water. He wondered, "Where did they come from? Of course! They came from the myriad of bubbles, bursting at the top of the froth on the tray! And what had George told him about bubble films? The surfactant is concentrated 100's or 1000's of times in the bubble film, compared to the concentration in the liquid as a whole. Suppose each drop of mist moving upwards did contain, oh, 100 times the concentration of surfactant in the feedwater? Now, suppose the upward water flow in the mist was, say, slightly more than one hundredth of the water moving downwards. Damn! The surfactant would move UP the tower, and would concentrate on the top tray! Now here was a potential concentration mechanism! And he already knew, from that otherwise useless isokinetic probe they had installed, that the water flow entrained in the gas could be 1% or more. His mind began to work feverishly. Yeah, it explained all the facts he knew. If the tower was stable, it would need only a minuscule, unmeasurable, increase in the feedwater surfactant to cause the tower to foam. After all, there were sixty-five trays in the cold tower, and that could magnify the effect tremendously. In that little test CGE had run with H_2S and Landrie Lake water, which showed it wouldn't foam, they had recirculated the water. As George said, a constant fresh supply of water was needed to concentrate the surfactant to a level at which foaming would begin. His mind began to struggle with the mathematics of the problem, and gave up. Shin-der could have a look at it tomorrow."

Look at it Shin-Der did, and soon came to Stan with his findings. If it was in fact happening, the concentration of surfactant on the top tray could be expressed by a mathematical term which included the Naperian Logarithm Base, 'e', or about 2.7, raised to the 65th power.

This could be an enormously large number. Putting it simply, the upward moving mist in the tower was only a small fraction of the water moving down. But if this upward moving mist was sufficiently concentrated in surfactant that it moved more surfactant UP than the bulk water could move DOWN, then concentration on the top tray was bound to occur. But, Shin-Der offered more, "You've set me to thinking," he said. "The foam height we measured on the top tray is a bit higher than Union Carbide expected, say 12 inches at the present gas flow. Our trays in the cold tower are only 16 inches apart. If the froth on the lower trays is the same height, then there is only 4 inches between the top of the froth and the bottom of the next tray. As we increase the flow, the froth height increases. Even a one inch increase in froth height will increase the water transfer upwards substantially. After all, it is only the smallest drops you can see moving upwards in the tower mist. There are lots of larger drops thrown off by bursting bubbles, which rise a few inches upward, and then fall back. I think we'd better measure the foam height in our towers."

A carefully monitored and controlled program of flow and pressure increases culminated in an extraction rate of about 85% of design, by the time of the summer shutdown. And then, using a novel technique developed by AECL, Shin-Der measured the froth height in C tower. A gamma ray source was lowered down one side of the tower, and a detector down the other. The gamma rays, just very energetic X-rays, penetrated the steel of the tower wall, but were partially absorbed by the water. Shin-Der came to Stan with the results the next day. "The froth height is about 14 inches. That's only two inches below the next tray. And that's not at full flow. To get the flow rate up to design, it will be necessary to lower the height of the outlet weir." But before any plans could be made to tackle this issue, Cape Breton labor was to provide the next unscheduled event.

9 STRIKE

Labor relations at the plant were never easy. There were a few employees, mostly in the maintenance department, who seemed to delight in twisting management's tail. Grievances, some real, mostly imagined, proliferated. Stan was reminded of his sister's description of the Welsh, among whom she lived for many years. "The trouble is," she said, "They were conquered by the Normans 850 years ago. They went into guerrilla warfare then, and they're still fighting. Since there is no longer any enemy, they have to invent one, even if it is themselves." Knowing his own country's turbulent coal mining and steel making history, Stan had no doubt there were plenty of real labour grievances in Cape Breton's past. But the local union officers were still inventing and fighting the battles of yesterday in a high tech industry of today.

One of Lee's first actions had been to get Phil, the CGE human relations manager who had been with the plant from the beginning, re-assigned back to Toronto, and then to replace him with a human relations manager more in his own style. Phil had been courteous, polite, formal, and always, always, 'proper', to use a somewhat archaic word. After a couple of replacements, also in the CGE style, Lee found Ian Davidson, a short stubby pugnacious Scot. He was cheerful, informal, and spontaneous, but when pressed, Ian could be stubborn and combative. He seemed to relish in the confrontational union/management situation he had inherited. Almost overnight, to the joy of most supervisors, who were, of course, on the front line, union relationships took a different path. No longer did management 'roll over and play dead' at every grievance. Now the union contract was interpreted literally, and disciplinary measures were enforced. Not surprisingly, the union did not like it.

There was more than one premonition of the trouble to come. One morning, the maintenance workers refused to enter the plant, and put up an informal picket line. The morning operations shift refused to cross the line. As Dave and Stan drove into work that morning, through the sullen line of scowling faces, several of the operations staff refused to meet their eyes.

Inside, Dave and Lee convened a hurried management meeting. "My night shift has agreed to stay at least till midday," Dave reported, "But, we can't keep them indefinitely. They've been here all night. The guys on the picket line are fools! Don't they know this is a hazardous plant we're running? And a shutdown would take days, and that is even riskier than just running. When this plant is steady, like it is now, it's easy to run."

And so the decision was taken. While Lee and Ian negotiated with the union, all salaried and professional staff were split into two operations teams. One team was sent home to get some sleep, with instructions to report back at 8:00 pm. The other team took over from the night shift about 10:00 am. Now the whole burden of safely operating the plant was placed squarely on about 40 people, only half of whom would be present at a time. The bulk of the GS process operators were now from the plant engineering group. They knew how the plant worked, what every piece of equipment was supposed to do, and while knowledgeable of emergency procedures, could hardly be called fully trained.

Fortunately, there were no problems and no emergencies. The only slight upset was, as often occurred at the plant, self-imposed. That evening, a routine laboratory test revealed that the 'pH' of the water clarifier needed adjusting. 'pH' is a measure of how acidic or alkaline the water is. It was controlled by a caustic 'metering' pump, a device which pumped a measured amount of caustic soda solution into the clarifier, proportionally to the water flow. Dave King had left strict instructions that no process variables were to be changed unless absolutely necessary. But water quality was important, and the engineer in charge of the water treatment plant that evening had designed and specified the pump involved. He was a quiet, diffident, elderly English gentleman, who never seemed to get angry or excited. He had a very slight stutter, which only served to enhance his impeccable English accent. The shift supervisor discussed the needed change with him. No problem, he knew exactly what to do, and went off to do it. About twenty minutes later, the effects of the change began to show on the control room instruments. There was only one problem. He had made the change the wrong way and the 'pH' was increasing instead of decreasing. The radio crackled to life, and he was instructed, in no uncertain terms, to put the situation right.

A few minutes later, over the radio, came his abject apology, in an accent recognized by everyone who heard it, "Oh d-d-dear. I t-t-turned the p-p-piston gauge the w-w-wrong way. So sorry. I really f-f-f****ed that up, didn't I."

This first, illegal strike involving CGE employees rather than construction union personnel was soon over. With the plant still operating, and the gas hazard in no way diminished, the union was in an impossible position, and Lee and Ian had no trouble driving home the legal problems they faced. The next morning, all was over, the picket line vanished, and normal operations resumed.

However, Stan got his wrist slapped. The Atomic Energy Control Board got wind of what had happened, and demanded to know why CGE had not shut the plant down. Stan had to explain at length how long it took to safely shut down a plant of this size, and how the very act of shutting down was, in many ways, more risky than continuing to operate it. Most importantly, a shutdown would never be attempted without a full complement of fresh operators, who were, of course, not available on this occasion. He had to agree that the Atomic Energy Control Board would, in future, be notified of any unscheduled change in the plant's operating status.

As bargaining progressed, in the spring of 1973, it was obvious no agreement was in sight prior to the end of the existing union contract. Most of the plant employees had, by now, worked four or more years continuously, with only their statutory two week vacations. For many, this steady work was a new experience, and bank balances were flush. For many, a summer strike would present an opportunity to visit family, renew old acquaintances, get some hunting and fishing in, and just relax. The manifest reason for the upcoming strike was wage rates, but most people just wanted a break. The union announced the legal strike, in advance, for June 21st 1973, and co-operated with management in the necessary plant shutdown. The last day before the strike was like the last day at school before the summer holidays.

For management and professional staff, it was not so easy. All vacations were cancelled, and four skeleton shifts were set up. With the plant shut down, operations were easy. Only water treatment and steam condensing, for Nova Scotia Power, were in use. But with gas still in all the towers, a small but real risk was present, and the new operations crews were drilled mercilessly by their supervisors in emergency and rescue procedures. There were also other things that could be done. Stan found himself assigned for a few days to the DW unit. Shut down, it was a deadly dull position, and his shift supervisor asked him to clean it up. Stan was mystified. How did you go about cleaning up a maze of catwalks, gratings and walkways? Patiently, the shift supervisor introduced him to phosphate, water, and a big power scrubber, and Stan got started.

The next night, a cartoon cut out of the Sunday paper was stuck up on the control room door. It showed a supervisor offering a broom to a new employee with the request to start by sweeping out the shop. The new employee is aghast. "Sir, you can't ask me to do that! I'm a PhD."

"Oh, sorry," replies the supervisor, "give it back here and I'll show you how it works."

The pickets on the plant road were not kind, even to those few professionals and supervisors who crossed the line to ensure the plant safety. Tacks on the road were a favorite device: Lee maintained he kept his old company in business that summer with replacement tires for all. Eggs were thrown, and cars damaged. On one occasion, Stan drove in with Dave Lillie, who had come up to discuss with Lee, Stan and his engineers the desirability of a weir cut. Roddy, a big burly pipe-fitter, and one of the few troublemakers on the plant, stopped them at the picket line. Stan, expecting no trouble, wound down his window. Roddy leaned his elbow on the door, and bent down for a better look. "Hello, my friend. And who might we have with us today?"

"Hi, Roddy. This is Dave Lillie, from GE. He's here to discuss some technical matters with us." Roddy's face worked enigmatically. He didn't like being addressed, cordially and as a buddy, by a member of the management team. Somebody crossing his picket line should show the appropriate emotion, if not fear, at least respect. And this manager, who he really didn't know at all, showed neither. It reduced his prestige as one of the strike leaders and instigators. But, he had a problem; this was clearly no strike breaking activity, and he had no valid reason to object. After a few moments, he straightened up and began to turn away. Then as Stan let in the clutch, Roddy whirled around and spat right in Stan's face.

Stonily, Stan drove in to the plant, cleaned up, marched in to see Lee, and told him what had happened. "Lee, if I bring a lawsuit against that guy, will the company back me?" Lee had been through several strikes in his career, but never one in which such unreasoning malice was directed, malevolently and capriciously, against innocent people. Moreover, he suspected this was going to be a long and spiteful episode, with no real winner at the end. He needed something to help maintain the moral of those folks who, at management's bidding, were stoically suffering this kind of abuse each day, just to ensure the safety of the picketers themselves.

"Tell you what," he said, "these guys have had it their own way long enough. I'm going to consult our lawyer to see if we can't get an injunction to stop picketing. Will you let me consolidate your event with others to show the union is being too aggressive?"

The subsequent 'trial', several weeks later, had all the elements of a kangaroo court in reverse. It was held in the tiny Port Hawkesbury court room, usually reserved for drinking and traffic offenses, in front of a small, pompous, dictatorial, judge. After hearing the evidence of people who had been verbally abused, barraged by eggs, suffered car and tire damage, and had been spat on, the judge denied the requested injunction to prevent picketing. He commented, "A big company like CGE clearly has the resources to control entry to its own plant. I'm not satisfied that CGE is doing all it can to end this dispute, and denying the right to picket may prolong it. I urge CGE to return to the bargaining table."

Not all such minor battles went to the union, and in a small way, one of Stan's experiments helped. At the manway at the top of C tower, just before the strike, a remote TV camera had been installed, looking into the tower. The control room operator could see the tray operation, and get even earlier warning of foaming than was provided by the delta P instruments. The electrical supervisor had the bright idea of turning this camera to face the entry road. Now control room staff had a bird's eye view of events on the picket line. If things seemed to be getting ugly, and an individual was outnumbered and being harassed on the line, reinforcements could be sent out from the plant, a small comfort to those individuals crossing. It made it seem not quite so lonely out there to know someone in the control room was watching out for you. One day, AECL sent in a truck to collect some of the product which, previously produced, was sitting in the DW unit. The pickets did their best to dissuade the driver from entering the plant, while Lee and Dave went out to the line to persuade him otherwise. A cheer went up in the control room as Lee swung himself up into the cab, and the truck drove through. Then the watchers had the extra bonus of seeing Roddy stamp his foot in frustration.

Finally, with the summer coming to an end, negotiations resumed, and the strike was soon over. Most supervisors maintained CGE settled too early, and the strikers should have been left out there for at least a taste of winter. But other forces, of which the plant staff was ignorant, were pushing Lee towards a settlement. He had to show real progress in licking the plant's problems. The decision to cut the weirs, once the strike was over, had already been made. AECL had bought the rights to use the Port Hawkesbury design from CGE, and had entered an agreement with Ontario Hydro, who were building several almost identical GS units to supply heavy water to their own nuclear power plants. The first of those Ontario Hydro plants had started up last year, and like the Port Hawkesbury unit, showed similar, although not so severe, problems. Lake Huron was a rocky, stable lake, and the water was relatively low in organic material. But the Hydro plants, being built a few years after Port Hawkesbury, had capitalized on the experience. The weirs were thin sheets of stainless steel, bolted into place, and easily adjustable. Ontario Hydro, closely following the Port Hawkesbury experience, was able to lower the weir heights quite early in 1973. The success of this modification was now beyond any doubt.

The Port Hawkesbury weirs, however, designed much earlier, were one inch thick plate, welded immovably into the structure of the towers. So once more, the towers were freed of gas and opened for maintenance work. Once more, uncomplaining Cape Bretoner's climbed into the towers, and wriggled up the tray manways, this time carrying flame cutters and grinders. The weirs at the side of the towers could only be reached by lying full length on the tray, with bolt heads digging painfully into the flesh. How anybody could operate a flame cutter or a grinder in those conditions was beyond Stan's understanding. But operate them they did, and slowly the work proceeded, even though, to Shin-Der's exasperation, the cut was not always as smooth and level as he wished.

Towards the end of this period, Stan bumped into Don Nazzer at Sydney Airport. Don seemed to have forgotten, or at least forgiven, the circumstances of their last parting. They chatted effusively for a few minutes as Don's plane prepared to board. "So, how's the plant doing?" Don wanted to know. "You seem to have had your share of troubles. Is the strike over? And did you ever find out what's limiting production?"

"Yeah, the strikes over," replied Stan. "And we've found the problem. The outlet weirs in the cold tower trays are too high."

Don was instantly 'all ears', "What do you mean, the outlet weirs are too high? They're the same as Savanah River."

"No," replied Stan. "Of course, Savanah River has bubble cap trays, not sieve trays like ours. But their outlet weirs are 2.5 inches, while ours are 4.5 inches. We're in the middle of cutting them now."

"No, that can't be." replied Don. "I would never have let that happen." And he turned on his heel and strode away to catch his plane, leaving an open-mouthed Stan raging helplessly in the middle of the floor, with visions of the pile of scrap metal from the weir cutting operation floating in his brain.

10 MATURITY FOR SALE

One October evening in 1973, Lee and Stan were in the control room when the first tower went back on line with the lowered weirs. The tower was started up modestly, at about 75% design rate, with the ultra-pure water of the 'carbon trial'. Now the ultimate proof of all the last 18 month's work was at hand. If this didn't work, there was nothing more Stan could think of to do. He hovered nervously around the premium foaming indicator, the top trays 'delta P', installed as the first effort of his task force a year ago. Out of all the task force's experiments, this had proved the most reliable; it was now even enshrined in an operating procedure with instructions what to do when a foaming indication appeared. As the water began to flow down the tower, the signal came off the zero, and then... and then... and then began to show the unmistakable signs of foaming! Stan was shattered. He turned away from the control room panel with tears springing to his eyes. But Lee brought a more mature judgement. "Hey, Stan, relax and wait a bit. These towers are probably filled with crap, artificial and human. There's cutting oils, metal chips, grinding paste. And I bet those guys didn't always come out to relieve themselves. We may have steamed them out, but that doesn't mean we got them clean. Let's see what happens."

As in many things involving judgement, Lee's perception was better than Stan's. The tower settled down within the hour. Over the next few days, the entire GS process went on-line. Over the next few weeks, the pressure and flow rates were increased to their design values. Wonder of wonders, the process hummed along like a well-oiled sewing machine! Stan's team collectively held their breaths as the winter deepened and the annual lake turnover occurred. No problem. They had really done it. Realization came slowly to all. The emotional response seemed muted, suppressed, deadened and anticlimactic. There was no single defining moment or event on which they could focus. The plant still had to be run for many weeks before production could be expected to increase to its design value. The inevitable equipment problems continued. A control valve stuck, a flowmeter began to read wrong, a sample line hydrated, a heat exchanger fouled with sulphur, a compressor seal system failed, and so on. Each of these minor problems had a deleterious effect on extraction. The clarifier gave some problems, which were finally traced to issues with the coagulant aid. There were numerous power and steam failures. The second stage, now operating at close to design throughput, showed minor foaming problems, and the third stage was found to have a number of damaged trays.

But finally, in early spring of 1974, came the first of many 'Five

Drum Days'. A pugnacious Lee walked into the control room late that afternoon, asking the operator's permission to use the plant loudspeaker system. "Now hear this," he barked into the microphone, in a fair imitation of the ship's captain he really was. "Now hear this. Today the CGE Port Hawkesbury Heavy Water Plant achieved its design production rate of 100lbs/hour. You are all to be congratulated!" Actual production, into drums, and billable to the customer, of 100 lbs/hr, had finally been achieved!

There were still plenty of events at the Cape Breton plants to keep everyone occupied. George, from Schenectady, came up for one of his last plant visits. He got into Halifax OK, but by the time he reached the Canso Causeway, about ten o'clock, a real Cape Breton north-easter was in full swing. A tractor trailer had jackknifed and blocked the causeway. The RCMP had closed it until morning. George phoned Stan, who was just getting ready to go to bed. "Stan, the causeway is closed, and there isn't a motel bed within a hundred miles. Folks are getting ready to sleep on the Keddy Motel dining room tables. I may have to drive back to Truro or Halifax."

Stan had a brain-wave. "George, if they've only closed the road, I bet the rail is still open. There is a little two car rail-liner that comes through soon after midnight. Get that, I'll pick you up on this side, and you can stay here. We've got room." So George's expense account for that trip showed no motel, and the grand sum of $1.50 for rail fare.

But the plant could still bite. On one particular Saturday, Stan happened to be Duty Manager. The Duty Manger served from 8:00

am on Monday morning to the same time the following Monday. He was provided with the emergency vehicle, a radio equipped Jeep. Stan was on-call for the shift supervisor, and was expected to take any management actions which an emergency situation demanded. It was Stan's practice, when on call, to drop in over the weekend and check how the process was running. The shift supervisor, Wayne, informed Stan that a 'blank' was being removed. The 'blank', a four inch diameter plain disc of metal, had been installed earlier, between the relief valve and the flare header, to isolate a heat exchanger from all possible sources of H_2S. Now that the heat exchanger was going back in service, the blank had to be removed. This was a 'hot' job, since the flare header was known to contain H_2S, but at a very low pressure. The procedure was quite simple. The four bolts holding the valve flange to the flange on the two inch diameter pipe leading to the flare header would be removed, the blank dropped out, a new gasket installed and the bolts reinstalled and tightened. For the few minutes in which the flare header was open to the atmosphere, both maintenance technicians would be wearing full face masks, connected by long flexible hoses to the piped breathing air system. There was only one minor complication; that the valve was about twenty feet in the air, on top of that heat exchanger shell. Scaffolding had been built to provide a rather cramped platform on which the men could work. The safety observer was to be the number two GS operator and his buddy, who would watch from the ground.

Stan was in the control room when the terse words, "We've got a man down" came across the radio. Almost simultaneously, the raucous sound of the 'Jesus Christ' alarm filled the air, indicating H_2S was known to be present. Within a very few seconds, two operators in emergency breathing air packs were racing down the hill into the GS area, carrying a stretcher, while other maintenance personnel began to leave. Shortly, the operators re-appeared carrying the body of Vince, with a resuscitator strapped to his face. He was carried into the little 'surgery', where Wayne and Stan shut the door on the anxious faces crowding around. Stan took Vince's pulse, and was relived to feel it strong and regular. Vince was unconscious, but breathing on his own. The emergency resuscitator was replaced with the oxygen supplied resuscitator in the surgery, and his color began to improve. Although unconscious, he showed the characteristic response of an H_2S gassing victim: if the resuscitator mask was removed, he would try to follow it with his nose, like a hungry man sniffing a steak. While waiting for the plant doctor to arrive, Wayne got the story from his operator.

"As far as I could see, he took his mask off to walk round the platform. He somersaulted through the air, landed on his feet, and collapsed. How he missed all those pipes on the way down was a miracle."

"You're sure he didn't have his mask on when he hit the ground?" Wayne asked.

"Positive," was the reply. "It's still up on the scaffold."

"And what about that flare header pipe?" Wayne inquired.

"It's still open, as far as I know," indicated the field operator.

Wayne stuck his head out of the door and gave orders for the pipe flange to be closed. How he could remember that in the midst of all the other confusion, Stan never knew. Shortly, the doctor arrived on site, and at about the same time, the pipe was finally closed, and the alarm switched off. Stan's panic level began to subside.

The doctor examined the still unconscious Vince, and came to a decision. "There's no injury I can see, but I don't really know what happened in the fall. He seems to be stable. Let's load him in the ambulance and ship him off to the Antigonish hospital. Can you spare somebody to ride with him and watch the resuscitator?"

Vince recovered consciousness in the hospital and was released after a short observation period, fully recovered. He had to be the luckiest man alive. If any part of his anatomy had hit a pipe on the way down, anything could have happened, from a broken leg to a broken neck. And landing on his feet was certainly not something to be expected from a conscious man falling twenty feet, let alone an unconscious one!

As senior management representative on site, Stan was asked to report on the event to the plant safety committee. Vince's story was that his mate asked him to remove a piece of torn plastic covering which was flapping in his face and no-longer providing the intended shelter. To do so, Vince had to walk round the platform. He did not remember anything else; specifically he did not remember removing his mask. The union made a halfhearted attempt to claim the mask was faulty and that Vince became unconscious and fell before he removed it. But it was obviously removed on the platform, else it would have fallen with him until the air hose caught and broke. It was not obvious to Stan why the union would go through that charade. Did they think poor Vince was going to be disciplined? He had already had been given the sharpest lesson a man could have and lived to tell the tale. He probably removed the mask in an almost unconscious gesture as he walked round the platform. Stan did not think he would do it again soon.

Roy Beaton called one day to say he wanted to come up and see Lee, and the plant production data, but that his corporate jet had been preempted by other, presumably even more exalted, GE management. He was going to fly on commercial airlines to Sydney. Since his time in Port Hawkesbury would be limited, he asked Stan to pick him up, so they could chat about technical stuff as they drove. Stan liked these precious moments alone with a Corporate VP; it somehow confirmed his special status and Roy's penetrating questions were sure to flush out any weaknesses in Stan's logic. He checked a company car out from the lot, one of the unpretentious Pontiacs, and drove northwards through the worsening weather.

Roy's flight was delayed, but at about 4:00 pm, Stan met him in the baggage claim area. "Hi, Roy. I'll go and get the car and meet you here. It's miserable outside." About 15 minutes later, Stan returned and picked up one of his bags, saying, "OK. Let's go."

"What took you so long?" Roy asked conversationally.

"Oh, it's icing a bit out there, and I had trouble getting up the hill." Stan replied breezily.

Roy stopped in the doorway, his eyes narrowing as he scanned the unfamiliar Sydney parking area, "What hill? I can't see any hill."

"Well, it's not really a hill," Stan replied evasively, pointing at the parking lot exit. "There's a little incline over there, out of the parking lot up to the road."

Roy regarded Stan speculatively, "So, what did you do?"

"Oh, after I'd tried to get up a few times front-wards, I managed it in reverse," replied Stan.

"Stay here and watch the bags," Roy said authoritatively. "Where's the car?"

Stan pointed it out to him and he marched out to carefully inspect each tire. "You mean you drove that thing out of the lot without checking the tires?" Roy said severely as he returned. "They're absolutely bald."

"The weather wasn't as bad when I left this morning," Stan replied miserably.

"Go and park it again. And be careful you don't hit anything. Then meet me by the rental desk," Roy ordered.

Stan met him there a few minutes later. Roy was having an animated conversation with the rental clerk. Conversation finished, he turned to Stan, "There will be slight delay while they find me a car with new snow tires. Who looks after your cars?"

"Err, Ted McEwan, finance." Stan replied nervously.

"I thought so. I have a standing agreement with my wife that if I am ever killed or seriously injured while driving a company car, she is to sue GE for every penny she can get," said Roy.

The next morning, Stan picked Roy up at 7:30 am. As they walked in the door, Roy said ominously, "Show me Ted's office."

Ten minutes later, a red faced Ted stormed into Stan's office. "Jesus Christ," he raved, "What are you doing to me?" Stan tried not to smile as he told him what had happened. Ted was not mollified, "He really reamed me out. Now what about that car in Sydney? When are you going to get it back?"

"Roy specifically told me that was your problem," Stan lied virtuously. "I think Roy is driving the rental back to Halifax. Why don't you ask him to return via Sydney? Then he can drive someone up with him."

"Do you think I need my head examined?" Ted grumbled as he left.

Roy, of course, was just teaching Ted and Stan a lesson in corporate standards. If you don't watch out for yourself, who will? And if you don't constantly strive for better performance for the company, who will? However, Stan suspected Roy's comment about his standing order to his wife was genuine.

Now, it was time to disengage the outside help. Schenectady actually took the initiative; Art was too good a manager to spend money where it was no longer useful. Despite the expenditure of several million dollars, Schenectady had not really done anything useful, either in the lab or at the plant, except for the most useful thing of all. They had provided a fundamental knowledge base and an expert discussion forum against which the plant site personnel were able to exercise their own judgment and sharpen their own arguments. The ideas which germinated at the plant would not have done so without Schenectady's directly relevant input, stimulating discussion, and comforting presence.

In the spring of 1974, several members of Stan's foaming task force were amazed to receive invitations to a party at Schenectady. The amazing thing about the invitations was, not only were they invited to travel at company expense for pure pleasure, almost unheard of, but that their wives were invited too, also absolutely unprecedented. At this party, for about a hundred people, held in the dining hall at the Corporate Research and Development Laboratory, two artistic endeavors were presented. One was a song, to the tune 'Clear Water', written by a nameless individual at Schenectady, and the second was a short comic play written by Stan. Both the words to the song and the script for the play are provided in the appendixes. Both artistic contributions seem rather puerile with the passing of time. Stan's contribution was written in about an hour, with almost no editing, obviously springing, spontaneously and mysteriously, from some deep well of relief. During the foaming problems, it was inconceivable that any such piece could have been produced.

AECL declined to suspend their research. Spending taxpayer money, it was easier to justify work of doubtful usefulness. At the peak of the foaming task force, in 1973, there were about fifty engineers and scientists working on GS and related problems at eight separate sites in Canada, and one in the USA. After the withdrawal of GE Corporate Research and Development team, AECL consolidated the effort into fewer sites.

Settling into routine operation, as spring approached, Dave King began to talk about the annual summer shutdown. Now Lee's real management skill showed itself. Without ever denying that a summer shutdown was necessary, he got Dave to compile and maintain a list of things which could only be done with the plant shutdown. Then, one by one, he began to challenge both Ted and Dave to either find ways to do the repairs without shutting down, or find ways to keep the plant operating semi-permanently with the defect. Dave did not realize what was happening until about June, when it finally dawned on him. He came into Stan's office grinning. "That cunning old bastard," he chuckled. "I suppose we can get by without a summer shutdown. Lee never intended to call it at all. But he let me talk myself out of it."

By now, Stan had summer sailing in Port Hawkesbury down to a fine art. His little 'Mirror Dingy', a fourteen foot gaff rigged pram, sat on a little home built trailer at the back of the yacht club, and could be rigged and in the water in about five minutes. Since it was five minutes from plant to home, and five minutes to change, Stan could actually be sailing a quarter of an hour after he left work. But haste does not always mean more speed. On this beautiful summer evening, as he pushed off from the beach, and tried to gather in the mainsheet, he realized it had caught round the rudder. The breeze was already stiffening the sail as he set out from the shore. "No problem," he rationalized, one hand on the boom and one on the tiller, "I'll just sail round into the lee of the jetty, come up into the wind, and then I can fix it." In the shelter of the jetty, he attempted a gibe, which rolled the boat over, and dumped both him and the dingy contents into the water. Gasping and spluttering in the cold sea, he collected the drifting bailer and cushion, and swam around to right the craft. Then he found the cause of roll-over. In the confusion with the mainsheet, he had neglected to fully lower the center board. He had been sailing with no keel when he attempted that gibe. He finally got the dingy righted and skimmed away into the sunset, the quintessential dingy sailor, wet, shivering and cold, but determined not to miss his evening spin.

The sailing club in Port Hawkesbury was, at that time, something of a misnomer, existing more for socials and dances than sailing. It did, of course, perform the important function of a licensed bar. The few full-sized yachts were typically put into the water about mid-June and taken out shortly after Labor Day. There were one or two traditional sailing events in between, but mostly the yachts swung to anchor.

A few days after his upset, Stan wandered into the control room where the shift supervisor was holding court. "A funny thing happened at the Yacht Club last Friday," related Jim Bray. "This grey haired old geyser sailed his dingy round into the sheltered water of the jetty, rolled it over, righted it, and sailed away. Why would anyone do that? Do you think he was practicing?" Stan had to admit who it was. He suspected Jim knew, and had started the story as soon as he spotted Stan.

The plant hummed along on its steady journey. The occasional gas alarm, usually now a drill, excited nobody. But the combination of experienced, slightly complacent operators, and H_2S, could still produce a surprise. Neil was a fully seasoned operator; his job one evening was to isolate a short length of piping, and purge it free of H_2S, to allow repair of a defective control valve the following morning. Although Neil knew what was required by heart, he was scrupulously following the written procedure, partly because it was what the top brass expected, and partly because it was easier not to have to think too hard about what to do next. The length of line involved was quite short, only about 40 feet, but, being 20 feet in the air, required a lot of ladder climbing. He and his buddy had closed the two block valves, one each side of the control valve, and opened the drain line to release the trapped water. Then they 'steamed' the line by connecting a steam hose to the vent, located at the top of the line, and flushed steam through to the drain. On this particular line, the drain was quite close to where the steam was introduced. Consequently, the steam did not easily reach all parts of the pipe, and Neil knew a prolonged steam might be required. The final step on the procedure read: 'Carefully open the vent valve to atmosphere and check for the absence of H_2S.'

"Huh," thought Neil to himself, "typical of those guys up in the office. That valve's twenty feet in the air. How do they expect you to do that carefully from a ladder?" Then he had an idea. He disconnected the steam hose from the low pressure steam header, leaving it connected to the vent. Now he could check for gas safely at ground level. "Right," called Neil to his partner on the ladder, "crack that vent." Instead of holding the hose well away from him while he checked with lead acetate paper, Neil sniffed the open end. When his partner turned round, Neil was prostrate on the ground.

Racing to the nearest rescue station, as standard emergency procedures dictated, his buddy rang in the 'Jesus Christ' alarm, and he was soon joined by a pair of oxygen bearing operators carrying a stretcher. Breathlessly, the buddy led them back to where the incident had occurred, and stared around bewildered. "But Neil was lying right here," he said incredulously, "Look, there's the hose."

They finally found Neil wandering bemusedly among the compressors on the other side of the towers. He forcefully resisted their efforts to lay him on the stretcher and administer resuscitation. But eventually, as memory penetrated his addled brain, he did consent to sit on the tailgate of the emergency truck, and take a few breaths of oxygen. It was a long time before his friends allowed him to forget the gassing victim who walked away from his rescuers and fought them when they found him.

Now Stan began to get bored. The routine of steady production was really not his cup of tea. His engineers had worked out a 'daily report', a computer program which took the regular measurements of deuterium from all stations in the process, estimated both the deuterium extraction by the first stage towers and the entire inventory in the process, and, by knowing how much product had gone into drums, was then able to show an 'MUF', or Material Unaccounted For. This should, of course, be zero, but rarely was. The laboratory deuterium measurements were good, but the first stage feedwater flows were only accurate to a few percent. And the inventory estimates were just that, estimates. The result was that the MUF really only meant anything when the plant had been running steadily for at least a week, and even then it had to be taken with a grain of salt. Stan knew all that, as did Lee, but Lee wanted to see the report every day, rain or shine, steady state or start-up. If Stan's engineers didn't run the report when they felt it was meaningless, Stan would get into trouble with Lee, which on one or two occasions ended in a public shouting match. Stan would go and apologize afterwards, because he knew that Lee was trying to inculcate in everyone a greater regard for the product on which their paycheck depended. But the trouble was, Stan's heart just wasn't in it. Another December rolled around, and again there was no foaming problem. He hardly got excited when, in January 1975, he was able to report 324 tons of production in 1974. Extraction was averaging over 80% of design.

Soon the speculation began. CGE had a successful operation, if not a profitable one. What would they do with it? The trouble was the contract negotiated with the government back in the mid 1960's had a declining price with time. Declining, you say? That's right. Product in the first 1000 tons or first 2.5 years of the contract would be bought at $20.50 per pound, the next 1000 tons or 2.5 years at $19.25 a pound, and so on. There was adjustment for 'force majeure' events, a euphemism for strikes, but the price would soon be down to $18.50 a pound. And oil prices were just starting their upward spiral, so energy costs were inexorably rising. Why would anybody, especially a traditionally fiscally conservative operation like CGE, sign on to such a deal? Rumor had it that the chairman of AECL, back in the 1960's, needed CGE's help desperately, but the Canadian government was somewhat anti-industry at the time, especially American industry. When CGE balked on the contract terms for escalation, which was the most discussed item in the whole contract, the chairman made a personal appeal to his opposite in CGE, promising he would set it right when full production began. With their lucrative business in components for Canadian nuclear projects, CGE could not afford to oppose a prime customer, and acceded to the contract with its trivial escalation clause. Now, of course, things were different. The two original parties to this verbal agreement, in both AECL and CGE, had retired. And Ontario Hydro had built two replicas of the Port Hawkesbury plant, powered with cheap nuclear fueled steam and electricity. They had taken advantage of CGE's Port Hawkesbury experience, and were already, with lower weirs, operating beautifully. The shortage of heavy water, so desperate for the Canadian nuclear program just a couple of years ago, was rapidly evaporating.

Unbeknownst to plant staff, the new chairman of CGE was not enamored with heavy water production. How could he be? With salaries, energy, supplies and overhead costs to be added, the plant was never profitable. CGE was to be paid somewhat more than $30M for its product over the next five years of planned plant operation. Even in the best year, 1974, revenue was about $12.5M, while providing a positive cash flow, but hardly providing a great return on the investment, now approaching $120M. So, in 1973, CGE secretly broached the Canadian government with the idea of selling the plant.

AECL was hardly enthusiastic. They had only recently acquired control of the Deuterium of Canada plant at Glace Bay, and were just coming to realize how extensive the necessary redesign and refit would be. However, nor were they completely opposed. There would be obvious economies in joint management and operation of the two Nova Scotia heavy water plants, not to mention combining R&D and technical know-how. CGE had just spent a million dollars in cutting the weirs, and by early 1974 it was clear the operation had been a success. CGE was offering a sweet deal. The plant had been completely depreciated already, so the sale would be taxable income. CGE were prepared to take an installment deal, in which the first year's payment would roughly equal the tax payable. That way, there would be no net effect on federal revenues in the year of sale. Subsequent payments could then come from revenue from the operating plant. The final sale agreement was for $63M, $30M in the year of sale, with the remaining $33M spread out over the next ten years.

In the spring of 1975, the bombshell fell. CGE announced it would sell the plant to AECL, hook, line and sinker. AECL would acquire the whole caboodle, land, equipment, and personnel, as an operating entity. There was instant personnel pandemonium. Everybody at the plant was offered a job, but most people had not been 'sold' before, and instinctively and understandably, didn't like it. The new employer and the old employees were, of course, locked into a symbiotic relationship.

Neither could function without the other. There was no

comparable work to be had within a hundred miles, so the employees were stuck. And AECL could not operate the plant without them. There was a six week notice period given; an employee's two choices were to find a new job and resign from CGE, or accept employment with the new boss.

Not surprisingly, almost everybody did the latter. There were a few exceptions. Lee, who had, of course, known about the deal all along, announced he would retire, and AECL appointed Bill Hatton, an Ontario Hydro manager, who had been resident at Port Hawkesbury for some time, as a replacement. That was a popular choice, since Bill was a well-known and respected figure. The CGE finance manager, Ted, of course returned to Ontario, to a traditional manufacturing entity.

Surprisingly, the one posting which really got Stan's goat was the treatment meted out to the human relations manager, Ian Davidson. Ian, apparently, was for once in his life outflanked by the union, who got their own early meeting with AECL management. Since AECL was also trying to start up the Glace Bay heavy water plant, with the same union entrenched, they were in no mood to continue the conflict management which had been a feature of Lee and Ian styles. CGE gave Ian a secure posting back in Ontario, with no real job, clearly just to get him out of the way.

For no obvious reason, Stan got enraged at AECL's kowtowing to the union. He had experienced no real union troubles, before or since the strike. His only unionized employees were the lab techs, who had caused no trouble whatsoever. Why then, put his own future on the line for a cause he could in no way influence? Perhaps the real reason was his waning interest in the job, as it had become routine, or being passed over by AECL for the Plant Manager's position, or just plain itchy feet. Whatever the cause, Stan announced he would not stay. Through his contacts with GE, notably Roy Beaton, he got himself a job in California. Unfortunately, visa formalities delayed his transfer. Bill, generously, allowed him to stay for several months as an AECL employee until those issues could be sorted out.

Since the plant operated continuously, AECL and CGE had to specify a date and precise time for the handover. Prior to the end of the appointed evening shift, CGE drained every drop of reactor grade product from the DW unit. It was the only time in the whole five years for which they had operated the plant that a partially filled drum was booked as billable product. "Render unto Caesar that which is Caesar's," thought Stan. The next day, AECL announced the price they would pay for reactor grade heavy water was to be increased to $36 per pound. As they were paying themselves, the whole purpose of this announcement was lost on the Port Hawkesbury staff. It appeared they wanted to rub CGE's nose in the dirt. The terms of the sale agreement were not public at the time and the need to generate more revenue, albeit artificial, internally generated revenue was not apparent. It appeared AECL wanted to be able to show they could run the plant profitably, and at $36 per pound, most Port Hawkesbury staff thought, anybody could. Almost immediately, staff increases were authorized, building upgrades were announced, and extra safety facilities were planned. Even a paved tarmac was approved for the GS area. With taxpayer money, it was apparently easy to justify things which CGE had managed without. The straw which broke the camel's back for Stan, was the parking lot flagpole. Lee had lobbied CGE for years to put one in as a morale booster for the staff, always denied as a luxury inappropriate to a plant in financial difficulties. Now one appeared almost overnight. Stan could hardly wait to leave.

11 CLIMAX

Now that Stan had decided to leave Canada, the last summer passed in a hazy, rosy, glow. Work was no longer a challenge, a total absorption, an excitement which occupied every working minute, as it had been in the good old days of Lee. Bill was cordial and supportive, but he knew Stan's attention was waning. Now, social happenings, bridge, sailing and poker were the events to which he looked forward, with the big move to the USA overshadowing everything else for his family. Joy had started a summer/fall Sociology class at the community college, even though they would probably leave before she could finish.

Shortly after AECL took over, the long awaited summer shutdown had begun, deferred a year by Lee's equivocation with Dave. But Stan had little interest in the interminable planning, sequencing, and scheduling of work to be done. His colleagues sensed his preoccupation and, understandingly, left him largely to his own devices. Towards the end of the shutdown, Dave sought his advice. "Stan, this is a safety matter, and I'd like your opinion," he began. "You know we've been repairing the high pressure flare tank, using the low pressure flare while we're shut down. And you know the repairs have taken longer than expected." Yeah, Stan knew. The operators had been having some trouble with water level control, and one of his guys had been working with them. Looked like a plugged drain line somewhere. "Well," Dave continued, "we've now reversed the flares. The high pressure flare is back in operation, and the low pressure flare tank is isolated for repairs. Winter's coming, those repairs are going to take longer than we thought, and I want to get going. Can we start up like that?"

Stan stifled a yawn. "Don't see why not. As far as I can see, the low pressure flare is only to ensure proper burning of small gas releases. The high pressure flare is the real safety device, and you've got that back in service. I'll get it checked out." Nobody could think of any reason why the safety of the plant would be jeopardized with this mode of operation, and the startup proceeded. A strike at the power plant was no problem; their professional staff seemed to be running it fine. By mid-September the GS process was up and running again.

Wednesday night was Stan's favorite, the weekly poker game. Since he was duty manager this particular week, he picked up the players and drove them to Gerry's house. It seemed only fitting to use AECL's emergency vehicle for an event which gave so much pleasure to half a dozen of their staff. And anyway, for the week Stan was on call, he had to take it wherever he went. The game went its usual raucous, joking, bluffing way, and about 1:00 am he drove everybody home.

"Duty manager to control room," he intoned on the radio as he turned down his road. "How are you guys running tonight?"

"Hello, Stan," the familiar voice of the control room operator responded, "We're fine. Steady as a rock. Do you want to speak to George?"

"Nah. Just tell him the game's over and I'm back home."

"OK. How did you do?"

"Not too bad, made a buck or two. I think Dave had a bum evening."

Parking the big 4 wheel drive vehicle in the driveway, Stan bounded up the three steps to his front door. "Damn," he swore to himself, "Joy's locked it. And my own keys are inside, since I've got the company wagon. Have to try the back door." Turning on his heel, he took a giant stride over all three steps, and collapsed in agony with a twisted ankle, as his foot came down sideways in a gopher hole. Rolling about on the lawn, clutching his stabbing foot in anguish, and trying not to scream, his first thought was, "Jesus, I hope none of the neighbors are watching. They'll think I'm drunk."

Hopping to the back door, thankfully open, and crawling upstairs, he took a few aspirins. These, with the beer he had consumed, sufficed for a few hours of drugged sleep. The next morning, to drive was impossible, and he called Dave and explained. "Yeah, I'll pick up the emergency vehicle today," Dave said, commiserating. "But, someone else will have to take it Friday night."

"I should be OK by then," Stan said with more confidence than he felt, "After all, I'm certainly not going anywhere this weekend." Joy drove him in to work, and the plant nurse strapped him up. But the plant doctor, fearing a fracture, sent him for X-rays. They were, thankfully, negative.

Friday night, Dave dropped the emergency vehicle off in Stan's drive. "You're sure you're OK?" he asked. "I'll be back Saturday night."

"I think I could drive if I had to." Stan replied. "And I'm only going to sit here and watch TV. I'll be OK, bored but OK."

It was still dark when the phone rang Sunday morning. Stan struggled awake and groaned as he eased his still aching ankle to a new position. When he picked up the phone, George's confident voice came over the wire, "Stan, we've had a total loss of steam from the power plant. We're in standby operation."

"Jesus," Stan grumbled, "What's the time?"

"It's 5:00 am. Wait a minute. That's the power plant calling now. They're talking to John….. Oh Great! They're ready to come back up again. 50,000 lbs/hr in ten minutes," reported George.

"Do you want me in?" Stan queried, willing a negative reply.

"Not unless you want to. I've called Dave and he's on his way in." replied George.

Stan hung up, and Joy mumbled sleepily as he wriggled back down into bed and closed his eyes. Dozing, he began to fantasize about his new life. "Was California really all it was cracked up to be?"

One of the secretaries had been distraught when she heard where they were going. "Oh, Mr. Davies! That's where they have those terrible earthquakes. Aren't you scared?"

That's what Stan had asked Gerry when he walked into that H_2S cloud. "Was that really four years ago? Why didn't the unknown scare him, as it did some people? Why he did he see it as an adventure?"

Complaining about the monotony of life, one of his twin daughters had once said, "It's OK for you! You went through the war!"

Stan wondered, "Did he really seek risk? Surely not. Did he crave change and excitement? To that he had to plead guilty." His reverie was interrupted by a distant explosion which rattled the bedroom windows.

Forgetting his ankle, he sat bolt upright in bed and called the plant. The tremulous voice of an obviously scared security guard answered. "Atomic Energy of Canada."

"This is the Duty Manger. Is everything OK out there?" Stan questioned.

"I dunno, sir. A tank has exploded and now it's on fire."

"Tell the shift supervisor that I'm on my way. And start the emergency call-in right away" Stan ordered.

He rolled a wide-eyed and protesting Joy out of bed. "Come on, love. I'm not sure what I've got to do and I'm not sure my ankle will stand up. You're driving."

"That big thing," she grumbled, "I hate manual gear changing."

Dawn was breaking as they rolled down the driveway and he grabbed the radio, "Control room. Duty Manager. What's going on?"

George's voice came over the air, no trace of panic that Stan could detect, "TS561 has exploded and is burning. The top has gone altogether. All personnel accounted for. We're starting firefighting operations."

"OK. Any gas release?" asked Stan.

"I can't tell. None of our perimeter alarms have rung in," replied George.

"I'll check the road," informed Stan.

TS561 was a low pressure, sour, intermediate product storage tank, about 30 feet high and 50 feet diameter. It was not directly connected to any of the high pressure gas systems, so there should not be much gas, even though it was the biggest tank on site. But how had it exploded? There should only be a few inches of water gauge pressure in it. As they came over the hill, he checked the wind direction by the pulp mill plume. So far, so good, a gentle wind from the northwest, carrying their steam down the Strait, out to sea. Thankfully, any gas release would also be carried away from the town.

As they rounded the corner, the plant came into view. TS561 was indeed burning, with the characteristic blue-white H_2S flame. A thin white plume, probably SO_2 and steam, rose from it and drifted to the southeast. Two fire monitors were already playing their jets on adjacent equipment. He had Joy stop the Jeep, and standing on the running board with his one good foot, tested for H_2S with the handheld Draeger sniffer. It read zero, as he expected. Two cars coming up behind, seeing him stopped and sniffing for gas, stopped also. The lights of more cars appeared behind them. He waved them on and into the plant, and told Joy to drive round the public road to the south. As they came by the H_2S loading area, the full extent of the damage could be appreciated. The roof of TS561 had vanished completely. He could see fragments of it both inside and outside the fence. It had been connected to the low pressure flare by a twelve inch gas pipe. This pipe was now hanging into the tank, its open end out of sight.

A few irresolute pickets were standing by the entrance to the Nova Scotia Power plant property. Stan told Joy to drive over. "Are you guys OK," he asked.

"Yeah," answered the ringleader, "but is it safe to stay here?"

"Look," Stan replied, "that plant's obviously in trouble. And the situation hasn't stabilized yet. At the moment, there's no gas and the wind is blowing away from you. Who knows what will happen in a few minutes. I'd advise you to go home." They began to argue amongst themselves, torn between a Cape Bretoner's duty to his union, and fear for their own hides. Stan directed Joy to a little knoll, where the construction camp had once stood, almost directly downwind of the still-burning tank. The white plume drifted overhead, almost invisible against the sullen clouds, and the acrid smell of sulphur dioxide hung in the air. Now the Drager gas tester still showed zero H_2S, but one part per million SO_2.

Turning, they drove back along the south plant fence. The pickets were still there; obviously unionism had won out over their concern for their own skin. But shortly, a Royal Canadian Mounted Police car showed up and cleared them out.

Stan checked in, "Control room. Duty manager, here."

"Go ahead." came Dave's familiar and strangely comforting voice.

"There's no gas out here that I can detect, just a bit of SO_2. Nothing dangerous. What's your situation?" Stan inquired.

"We think the fire is being fed by H_2S leaking from the purge and stripper area. We're trying to find it and block it in." answered Dave.

"OK. You've obviously got enough help in there. I'm going home to drop Joy off, and then I'll be back," Stan reported.

They drove back, not round the by-pass, but through the still sleeping town. It was full daylight by now, but nary a sole did they see. "What did I expect," Stan wondered, "a milling crowd around the town hall, demanding protection?"

Their passage home was not unobserved, however. Later a nameless resident was purported to have exclaimed, "We knew it must be bad out there when we saw Mr. Davies driving away from the plant with his wife." So start rumors, but for all its insularity, Port Hawkesbury was not a town to be easily panicked.

Back at the plant, the situation was stable but still poorly understood. The pure blue-white flame was now mixed with black smoke; residual oil floating on top of the water had obviously caught fire. Dave came over to Stan fuming. "You remember we motorized the purge tower feed valve 'cause my guys hated running up there every shutdown and blocking it in? Well, we closed it from the panel here, and now we find it didn't close completely. So, the purge tower flooded and the relief valve lifted; that's been one source of sour water running into the flare header. Now we've got the purge tower blocked in, but it looks as though one of the other purge and stripper relief valves lifted and won't reseat properly. That's what's feeding the fire. The broken end of the flair header fell back inside the tank. We're flooding TS561."

"There's probably over a ton of product in there." Stan protested.

"I can't help that." Dave replied grimly. "We've got an open flare header. Suppose another relief valve lifted?" Stan had to agree.

One of Stan's engineers who had responded to the emergency call in sidled up to him. "Stan, should we get a dump on the data logger? It might tell us what happened." Glancing at his watch, Stan could have kicked himself. Damn, it was 6:45 am.

"Yeah. We've already lost the one minute averages. But you can get the five minutes," replied Stan. Computers were not as ubiquitous then, as they are now, and memory capacity wasn't as cheap. The data logger sampled every instrument in the plant at 20 second intervals, then averaged the last three readings as 'one minute averages' and stored them for one hour. After one hour, it averaged the last 5 readings as '5 minute averages', and stored them for 12 hours. At the end of the day, it stored the one hour averages permanently on magnetic tape. Had he been quicker on the ball, they might have caught the one minute averages for the critical time between 5:00 and 5:30 am. Now, they were now lost irretrievably.

At about 8:30 am the flare, which had been extinguished from the time the accident started, suddenly relit. TK561 had obviously flooded to a height at which the open end of the broken flare header was now under water. At the same time, the TK561 fire diminished sharply and turned into the rolling black sooty clouds characteristic of an oil fire.

The management team caucused briefly. "What happened?" was on everyone's lips, but Dave would have none of it.

"I just want you all to agree that we're going to be shut down for a long time. I'm going to hold the night shift operators over to join the day shift, and start blocking in the GS process. OK?"

The rest of the day passed in a blur of emergency meetings, discussions, and 'ad hoc' planning. About 4:00 pm, Bill called Stan into his office and asked, "Stan, you still haven't received your visa for the USA?"

"No, replied Stan, "I called them last week and they said they're still working on it."

"I'd like you to take charge of the investigation into this explosion," Bill asked.

"Why me?" Stan demurred. "I'm on one week's notice with you, and I'm quite likely to pull up stakes in the middle of it."

"I'll take that chance," replied Bill grimly. "It might get messy. I don't want any cover up on this one. If somebody blew it, I want responsibility placed fair and square. You have no reason to be sweet on anybody."

Stan hesitated. It meant diving back into the deep end. Twelve hour days, unrelenting pressure to produce, and perhaps management politics, which he hated. But, curiosity got the better of him again. He did want to know what happened. "How could a low pressure tank, connected to an open flare, explode?" he wondered. Besides, the sailing season was over. "OK," he sighed, "I'm on."

That night he got home as dusk was falling. The house seemed strangely quiet. No bustling in the kitchen and no appetizing smells of dinner cooking. The twins were downstairs watching TV and Joy was sewing in the sitting room. "Gosh, I'm beat. What a day. We were real lucky it wasn't worse." he exclaimed, hobbling into his favorite chair and reaching for the Sunday paper. "What's for dinner?" His ankle, forgotten in the early excitement of the day, was by now throbbing painfully again.

"I don't know what's for dinner." Joy replied quietly, head bent over her sewing. He glanced up at her sharply, but she seemed quite composed, almost preoccupied in the task at hand. Perhaps she was just finishing up, and she hated to be pulled away from something almost completed. Perhaps she was giving him a hard time for dragging her out that morning. He decided to relax a little and continued with the paper.

He broke the silence, "What's for dinner?" about 15 minutes later.

"I don't know. What's for dinner?" she responded, continuing her sewing. He limped down into the recreation room to see the twins watching TV.

"Mum been OK today?" he asked them.

"Yeah," responded Sylvia, "perhaps a bit quiet this afternoon. When are we having dinner?"

"I'll find out." he responded grimly as he turned and trudged back up the stairs. "Joy, when are we having dinner?" he tried again.

"I don't know. When are we having dinner?"

Stan quite prided himself on never losing his temper. In the seven years at Port Hawkesbury, through all the trials, tribulations, disappointments and problems, it had happened only once before. His latest secretary, a pretty local girl, sat sobbing quietly at her desk. "What's the matter, Carol?" Stan asked.

"Oh Mr. Davies," she mumbled, "I asked Mr. McEwen to get me a new typewriter, like you told me to. He said there was nothing wrong with this one and I should learn to type. But the line space doesn't work properly, like I told you, and I can't do neat work." Stan walked round to Ted McEwen's office intending to ask, politely but firmly, why she couldn't have a new typewriter. The walk was about 150 feet. Strolling into Ted's office, he posed his question.

"Ah, you know these local girls" replied Ted. "Lee's secretary just got a new typewriter and now everybody's going to want one. Your secretary can manage with what she's got".

To the startled surprise of both of Ted and himself, he completely lost his temper. Swearing in humor was OK to Stan, but swearing in anger was completely foreign. "Look here, you ********!" he bellowed, pounding Ted's desk with his fist, "That *********** typewriter is broken. Get her another one, right now!" And a new typewriter appeared that afternoon.

Now Stan could feel his temper rising again, but he determined that this time, rationality and reason would win out. After all, this was his wife and they rarely argued, let alone quarreled or even lost their tempers. A calm discussion would soon sort out the problem.

"Joy, what's up? I'm sorry I got you out of bed to drive this morning, but nobody could have known what we would have to do."

"There's nothing up. I didn't mind driving," Joy replied.

"Then what's wrong. When are we going to have dinner?" Stan answered.

"I don't know. When are we going to have dinner?" Joy reiterated. Now he completely lost it.

"If you can't cook ******** dinner for me after a day like today," he raved, pounding the table with his fist, "I'll take the ****** twins out for a ******** hamburger. What's the ******** matter with you?"

"Don't swear at me. You don't have to go out," Joy responded primly, "I've got some dinner. It was my sociology class assignment."

His mind struggled to grasp her words.

"What?" he said stupidly.

"In my sociology class, she gave us all a homework assignment." Joy reported.

His mind still could not grasp her import. "A homework assignment?" he repeated.

"Yes. We have to report how our family reacts when the primary care giver acts completely out of character," Joy explained.

It began to penetrate. "You mean this was an act? You were putting it on?" asked Stan.

"Of course," she said, somewhat huffily, "Don't I always cook dinner?"

"But why today?" he roared, the adrenalin still surging through his veins. "With all I've been through, why today?"

"The report's due tomorrow," she said contritely, "and all week

I've been trying to think what to do. I was going to do it Thursday, then you sprained your ankle, and it didn't seem fair. Today was my last chance."

It was some time before he could forgive her and several hours before the real humor of the situation grew on him. "Well," he mumbled as they settled down to sleep that night. "I guess you got your reaction."

The next day, Stan began his investigation. It quickly became apparent that there were only two hypotheses which could account for what had happened. Either an oxidant had somehow gotten into the tank, creating an explosive mixture with the H_2S, or the tank was over pressurized in some manner. Both seemed highly unlikely. The tank was constantly purged with nitrogen with the express intent of excluding oxygen. And the tank was connected to the flare header, which in turn was connected to the flare stack, venting to atmosphere through a small water seal in the flare drum. Stan went about the investigation much as the National Transportation Safety Board explores an aircraft crash. Operators and witnesses were interviewed and process records were examined. The tank wreckage was even reconstructed, to disprove the hypothesis that instrument air was flowing into the tank instead of nitrogen.

The final explanation was, as usual for these types of events, a combination of many circumstances. The tank failed at a pressure of about 10 psi, a far lower pressure than would be expected, because of substantial corrosion at the roof-to-tank wall weld. The tank was over pressurized by the lifting of pressure relief valves in both the purge tower and the flash tank. The former was discharging large quantities of water to the flare header, and the latter was discharging gas. Because of the non-standard operation of the flare system, combined with a design error, the water delivered to the flare tank could not drain away fast enough. The relief valve was passing gas to the flare header therefore pumping water up the flare stack! At the time of the explosion, water had flooded the flare stack, which was four feet in diameter, to a height of about 20 feet, and was rising at about two feet per minute. The flare header pressure was, of course, increasing in sympathy. They had been far luckier than they had any right to be. If TS561 had not been corroded, and failed at the abysmally low pressure it did, sooner or later, something else in the flare system would have failed, with potentially much more serious consequences. Finally, the whole thing had started when it did because of those strikers outside the Nova Scotia Power plant. They had turned off the main oil feed to their plant, causing the total steam failure, and nearly being crushed by falling pieces of the TS561 roof for their trouble!

What a catalogue of errors. Blind and complacent management, in which Stan included himself, were lulled by the very routine of dangerous operations into accepting nonstandard procedures without adequate forethought. There was indifferent supervision, more concerned with minimizing work and keeping life simple, than with the true risks of their actions. And heedless unionism played a part – Nova Scotia Power union's intent on making their point without thought or knowledge of the consequences of their actions. There was enough blame to go around, but this time our plant union was the one blameless actor.

Shortly afterwards, Stan's visa for the USA came through and he left Port Hawkesbury for California. There was the usual farewell party, the usual jokes, japes and speeches. He was baptized with 'holy' water, in a complicated ritual which confused a small bottle of supposedly heavy water with deer urine. There were mementos: a glass model of the plant filled with oil, carbon black, and antifoam; a model schooner with the towers as masts; a stainless steel miniature drum of heavy water. He was given a beautiful picture of the Bluenose, close hauled under full sail. The party passed in a haze of memories, good fellowship, regrets and hopes. Then, in a moment, it was over.

For years after, in the calm of his sinecure GE job in California, Stan reported having twisted dreams of this period in his life. They usually involved the heavy water plant control room in some way… and he was basking in the glorious view of the Canso Strait.

Epilogue

Atomic Energy of Canada Limited ran both the Glace Bay and Port Hawkesbury Heavy Water plants until 1985. Heavy water is not a consumable product in CANDU reactors, so most of the demand for the plant's product comes from building new reactors. By 1985, Ontario Hydro was self-sufficient in its own heavy water production and the foreign demand for AECL's CANDU reactor had dried up. After the plant's permanent shutdown in 1985, the towers were scrapped and the GS site cleared, leaving only the Administration building which was converted for general industrial use. It still exists on the site today.

Appendix 1 A One Act Play

PORT SCHENECTADY - One act play, in four scenes, for two characters.

For the first time ever in print, the naked tensions and emotions latent in the scientific corridors of power in a large multi-national corporation are exposed to public view. The facts are real. To protect the innocent, only the names have been changed.

THE CHARACTERS:

The Port Hawkesbury Engineer for Water (PHEW):

A slightly disheveled character, usually wrapped up in 16 layers of warm clothing, but distinguishable in the office by the mud on his shoes. Invariably crisis ridden. Given to rather incoherent ranting and raving, which at the best of times is difficult to understand, since it is conducted in an elaborate letter and number code known only to the initiated. Invariably, thinks he knows his own problems, but it always turns out that he doesn't know the first thing about them.

The Corporate Research und Development Scientist (CRUDS):

Usually sports a tweed jacket and pipe. Always requesting more data, even when buried in mounds of irrelevancies. Always unruffled. Given to long pontifical statements which, when summarized, mean "we don't know". Operates in a very precise and controlled environment which bears absolutely no relationship whatever to the problem under investigation. Considers any operation of the plant slightly miraculous in the face of the glaring gaps in knowledge.

SCENARIO:

The action takes place in a variety of locations across the USA and Canada, varying from discussions outside "A" manway on "C" tower, to the country club atmosphere of the Savannah River Plant in South Carolina. The duration spans two years, from mid-1972 to mid-1974. In the interests of brevity, only the more pertinent remarks from the many long and involved conversations are given here.

PHEW: Help, help!! We have a foaming problem.

CRUDS: Please describe exactly your symptoms.

PHEW: First IM-370 and IM-392 increase and IM-391 decreases. Then IM-318 shows spikes; that is it increases and decreases at the same time. Then the L/G goes wrong, as shown by the MCC's. Then all the water moves instantaneously from the top of the tower to the bottom. Then AV-361 opens, followed by AV-663 and IM-100, 200, 300. Then...

CRUDS: Thank you. What do you propose to do about it?

PHEW: Well, it's all in the water, you see, so we're going to clean it up.

CRUDS: Any attempt to solve this problem by a complete chemical characterization of the water must be regarded as a most complex and challenging project with a highly problematical outcome.

PHEW: Do you mean it's impossible?

CRUDS: Any attempt to solve this problem...

PHEW: Thank you.

CRUDS: We will send a series of skilled observers to holida… I mean to assist you in elucidating you problems, which clearly only occur between July and October...

PHEW: Oh, no - they're much worse in winter.

CRUDS: ...and then we will be in a position to advise you further.

INTERLUDE

CRUDS: We are now in a position to advise you that you have a most complex problem.

PHEW: Yeah, but what's the surface tension?

CRUDS: A complete review of tray hydraulics is called for and we have retained an expert consultant...

PHEW: Does he know the surface tension?

CRUDS: who advises us that your problem is probably gas blowing back up the downcomers.

PHEW: Well, our review of tray hydraulics tells us that gas blowback is certainly not the problem. Anyway, we have some tray hydraulic tests coming off soon which will not answer that question, so we can ignore it. We really want to know what the surface tension is.

CRUDS: We have some novel techniques which will tell us if you are foaming by shaking water and listening to it. We want to listen to your towers.

PHEW: That's OK, but we can't let you shake them. Have you measured the surface tension yet?

CRUDS: No, no. We'll listen to the towers and shake the water in the laboratory.

PHEW: At great trouble and expense, back charged to you, we have attached microphones to the towers. Now what about that surface tension?

CRUDS: Our acoustic analysis shows you suffered a foaming incident at 3:10 am on the night of October 14th.

PHEW: Yes, our Delta P measurements showed it.

CRUDS: Ah, but our acoustic measurements showed it earlier.

PHEW: Why didn't you tell us earlier?

CRUDS: We were not sure.

PHEW: Have you shaken any of our plant water yet?

CRUDS: We have shake-tested distilled water, doubly distilled water, triple distilled deionized water, and sewage water. They all look the same.

PHEW: What about plant water?

CRUDS: Of the 468 samples of plant water dispatched to Schenectady, only two have arrived. One is unlabeled, and the other has a packing nail driven through the plastic container. We are currently running the packing material through the wringer. We have however measured the surface tension.

PHEW: Oh yeah. What for?

CRUDS: (Expletive deleted) The surface tension decreases as the pressure increases.

PHEW: That's interesting. We are thinking of treating our feedwater with activated carbon.

CRUDS: Yes, of course you need to do that just before the purge tower.

PHEW: No, it's too expensive and we can't sort out our design parameters in time. We are going to add it to the clarifier.

CRUDS: That's no good. It's the wrong place, and once you do it there, you'll never be able to get the money to do it in the right place.

PHEW: But, you don't want to do it in the right place. It works better in the wrong place. Anyway, it's more fun. You can see it working and Australians are coal miners by nature. We also want to cut the weirs. The originator of this proposal insists we proceed from top to bottom, rather than from side to side.

CRUDS: AAARGH! We are certainly not prepared to approve such a radical measure without a complete theoretical evaluation.

PHEW: We have given it to you.

CRUDS: We do not fully accept the fundamental scientific basis of your hypothesis.

PHEW: Give us your solution.

CRUDS: (Long silence).

PHEW: Perhaps we can persuade AECL to try it at Bruce.

CRUDS: Under those circumstances, we will give it our unqualified approval.

PHEW: The carbon trial is working beautifully.

CRUDS: (Sotto voice) It's in the wrong place.

PAUSE FOR STRIKE.

CRUDS: With the aid of a leading tray manufacturer, we have completed an exhaustive evaluation of sieve tray hydraulics.

PHEW: What conclusions have you drawn?

CRUD: Two. Firstly, we cannot complete an exhaustive evaluation of sieve tray hydraulics, because low pressure air water tests do not completely represent the plant conditions.

PHEW: And?

CRUDS: Working with fluorescein dye can cause your wife to glow in the dark.

PHEW: Bruce E2 is working beautifully with cut weirs. We should cut ours.

CRUDS: We agree. What about the second stage?

PHEW: Oh, we never have any second stage problems. We'll leave well enough alone.

CRUDS: We strongly recommend that you cut the 2nd stage weirs.

PHEW: (Inaudible)

PAUSE FOR WEIR CUTS.

CRUDS: How is the plant working now?

PHEW: Well, OK. However, our extraction efficiency is not so good. Perhaps we cut the weirs too much.

CRUDS: Apart from that, is everything else all right?

PHEW: Well, um, err, you see, we are having second stage problems.

CRUDS: Why?

PHEW: We think it's a foaming problem.

CRUDS: Why not use antifoam?

PHEW: We can't do that!!

CRUDS: Why not?

PHEW: We've never done it before. It will fill up the third stage with antifoam.

CRUDS: Well, I suppose you could cut...

PHEW: Antifoam works beautifully in the second stage.

CRUDS: In that case, we can all go home.

PHEW: You mean you're leaving?

CRUDS: That's right.

PHEW: Help, Help!! We have a problem!!!

THE END

Appendix 2 Heavy Water Song

Sung to the tune of "Clear Water"

Why did I roam
So far from home
To find some foam
On water.
Heav-y Water.

I cry big tears
In Schooner beers
And cut the weirs
For water.
Heav-y Water.

Though the Northland's nice,
It ain't paradise,
And I'll give you some advice;
Don't mix "frazzle" ice
With water.
Heav-y Water.

So up column A
In search of spray
And drown our dismay
In a Hawkesbury hydraulic tray.
With water.
Heav-y Water.

My heart goes thump
Just like a pump
To weep or dump
Some water.
Heav-y water.

Forget cruel fate
Let's innovate
Coagulate
Some water.
Heav-y water.

Appendix 3 Reflections of a Son

Stan had four children but, I took the most interest in the Heavy Water Plant. Reading Dad's book, 'Is Making Heavy Water Painful?', brought back memories of both my high school years and the two summers I worked at the plant while I was a university student. I heard firsthand many of the 'stories' which were a part of the culture of working at the plant. These are my reflections of those times – Ray.

The first time I heard of Cape Breton, or even Nova Scotia, was on a family camping vacation. We drove from Peterborough, Ontario to Cape Breton, stopping at the usual tourist spots along the way. Once we made it to Port Hawkesbury, we checked into a motel. Our family camping trip was now a business trip for Dad, as he went into the heavy water plant, still under construction at that time. On the return trip, Dad told us that we were moving to Cape Breton. Also, on that return trip, we stopped at Grand Falls, New Brunswick for lunch. We were all totally disgusted with the large amounts of foam forming as the polluted water crashed over the falls. There was so much foam, it was being blown around by the wind. Perhaps it was a sign of things to come.

I was soon living in D'Escousse with a manager on-call. Being on-call was not easy in the early 70's; with no cell phone or even a pager, Dad was tied to the house phone when he was on-call. I can remember Dad parking the on-call Jeep at the end of the D'Escousse wharf in the summer. The Jeep had a two-way radio which was just capable of reaching the plant's control room. This meant Dad could watch us water skiing from the wharf, but still cover his on-call duties.

I do not recall too many, "There is trouble at the plant, I have to go in" occurrences, except at Christmas. My first Christmas Day in Nova Scotia was marred by Dad being called into work. It became such a regular Christmas occurrence, that in later years, after we had moved into Port Hawkesbury, a seasonal tradition started. The plant managers went in for the 'Christmas Day management meeting' even though nothing was wrong; it was a chance to wish the crew on shift that day, a Merry Christmas.

Dad wrote of vacations being cancelled early on in the plant start-up. He failed to mention that Dad and I were scheduled to fly to England and visit his parents (my grandparents). His trip was cancelled and I flew to England alone that summer. This was memorable for me, as it was the first time I had ever flown alone.

As I got older, trips into the plant with Dad were a real treat. The first trip to that control room was both memorable and impressive, with its panoramic view of the Strait and close-up view of the plant towers. The lights, switches, controllers and paper strip chart recorders on the control panels would have impressed a kid of any age. One of those early trips to the plant was to see my first computer. I was sat down in front of a TTY (Teletypewriter) and a 'football' game was started. The TTY would rattle out the status of a simulated football game, typing out things like, "The ball is on the 34 yard line, 1st and 10 yards." When my team had the ball, the TTY would stop and wait for my next call, as the team's quarterback (pass, run, kick etc). When my team lost possession, the TTY would spit out the plays continuously, with the computer as the quarterback for the opposing team. Needless to say, I lost the game. The following day, I took the TTY printout to school to show a friend. He ignored the impressive technology and pointed out my poor call, "You called for a long pass on 3rd down with one yard to go?!?"

Dad was clearly impressed with the glass portholes installed on C tower, with the corresponding TV monitor in the control room. So, one summer evening, he asked, "How would you like to go in and 'see' the tower operating?"

I responded, "Will there be another opportunity? There is a dance at the rink this evening."

Dad answered, "Sure." However, I was doubly disappointed. First, the dance was cancelled and second, another opportunity to see inside an operating tower never materialized.

Dad's weekly poker games were a mainstay of his time in Cape Breton. Did these social get-togethers contribute anything to the well-being of plant operations? Notwithstanding Dad's twisted ankle, the games were a chance for managers and shift supervisors to chat informally. I went down to the basement one evening to hear a vigorous discussion on foaming during a game. Gerry was insisting that GE just had to find the right antifoaming agent. The foaming problems at Gerry's previous plant out west cleared up when they switched antifoaming agents.

As I was completing Grade 12, I was called into the plant for a summer job interview. The next day, at school, my friend asked how the interview went and congratulated me when I said I had a job. I was taken back by the congratulations as it was not an interview. It was more of a plant orientation and description of the job. As the son of a manager, I assumed there was no question that I would get the job. Soon after that, Dad informed me that there is going to be a strike at the plant, but it would not affect my summer job. Clearly, the management team was not expecting the animosity or the picket line tactics by the union. By the end of the first week of the strike, all summer student jobs at the plant were cancelled. This was based on the assumption that those students would probably wish to work at the plant sometime in the future, so it would be wise for them not cross the picket line. I ended up with a house painting job that summer, somewhat of a disappointment after the promise of a job at the plant.

The most interesting strike story I heard was from Dad. A labour arbitrator was brought in and talked to both sides before the strike. CGE had their bottom line number for an hourly rate increase, but the arbitrator advised CGE not to present it at that time, as the offer would be rejected by the union. The union wanted a walkout. By the end of the summer, the union had settled for $0.01 per hour more than CGE's pre-strike bottom line number. If things had gone down differently, would I have had a third summer at the plant?

So, off I went to university without the exposure to the engineering marvel of the heavy water plant. Dad's background was a pure physics degree, but he now found himself totally immersed in an engineering environment. Doug Mobley had impressed Dad with his knowledge and intellect, after coming to the plant with his Engineering-Physics degree from the University of British Columbia. So, it seemed like a good idea for me to head off to Dalhousie University to study Engineering-Physics.

The following summer I was hired on in early May to join Neil's steam tracing crew. Neil was the senior operator who had gassed himself, but who, famously, the rescue crew had trouble finding. Most operators were on shift, covering the continuous operation of the plant. Neil, well into his fifties, was given a day job of supervising a crew dedicated to the repair of leaks in the plant's steam tracing. This avoided the excessive paperwork associated with the plant's work permit system for each of the many small steam leaks. The crew consisted of operators to isolate the lines, a pair of pipe fitters to do the repairs, and a pair of labourers to fix the pipe insulation after the repair. Neil's buddy was an interesting guy, but first I should review the buddy system and explain the operator training program.

As explained by Dad, the term 'buddy' does not refer to your friend, but a co-worker paired for working in the areas of the plant where H_2S gas could be present. You and your buddy were mutually responsible for each other's safety, and therefore must be in close proximity at all times when out in the field. This compulsory buddy system means one worker could be standing around doing nothing if the task at hand was only a one-man job.

Operators were hired as 'Operator trainees'. Then, after some plant experience, an operator could write a test and become a Class 3 Operator. A suitably motivated operator could work up to a Class 1 in about 5 years, with corresponding pay increases for the more advanced classes.

Neil's buddy was still an 'operator trainee', even after a couple of years at the plant. He was on the day-shift for 'light duty' due to a back problem. For that first month of May, I never saw him do anything except chat with Neil and other people in our travels around the plant. Then one day, we were called up to the water treatment area to isolate something for maintenance. Neil found the required valve up on the ceiling and went off looking for a ladder to reach it. Meanwhile, his buddy realized, on his own initiative, the valve could be reached by standing on a pile of bags of water treatment chemicals. He climbed up, reached with an outstretched hand and closed the valve; the first thing I had seen him do in a month. The next day, he did not show for work because he was sick (sore?) and I never saw him again. Neil was never given another buddy that summer, and I am sure the 'buddy rules' were stretched a bit as Neil informally hung around with other members of his steam tracing crew.

One day, Neil and I were up the towers on the top catwalk. Like Dad, I would never turn down an opportunity to go up the towers. On a clear summer day, the view of that part of Nova Scotia was spectacular. And, in an eerie similarity to Dad seeing that transformer fire start from a tower catwalk, Neil and I witnessed a commotion 250 feet below at the plant substation. Two electricians ran out of the building, jumped into their truck and drove up the hill to the administration building. The hum from the large tower compressors stopped, a worrying sign. Neil said, "Yep, the plant has shutdown. They will be busy in the control room now... Oh shit!" Then Neil took off like a bat out of hell. If I thought Neil was given this day job because he was getting old and slowing down, I was wrong. Neil ran all the way to the end of the catwalk and, not waiting for the elevator, he took the stairs down. He had gotten to the second level catwalk (~100 foot level) when I caught up with him, and that was only because he had stopped running.

Then, Neil explained himself. There was a fountain of water spurting up in the air by the plant fence. This was caused by a large amount of water being discharged into the process ditch. Neil said this water is often 'sour'. He had seen a shift operator, who had the reputation of being careless and lackadaisical, walking towards that fountain alone without his buddy. Neil feared the operator was in danger of being gassed. The danger had passed, as the operator was now walking away from the fountain.

The cause of the plant shutdown was a fire in an electrical breaker when it was being put back in service. Later in the lunchroom, the word was the breaker was faulty, whereas, at home, Dad said the electrician had done something wrong. Irrespective of which was true, the electrician followed his training by shielding his face when racking in the breaker. He only received a small burn on his arm and was back at work in a couple days. To this day, I still look away when switching on a breaker at home.

My buddy that summer was Dan. Dan was an engineering student going into his final year at the University of Toronto. His father was both our next door neighbor and the plant manager at the Gulf Oil refinery, located next to the heavy water plant. Dan's father did not think it would be a good idea for the manager's son to work at the refinery. So, I am sure, Dan's job at our plant was a result of a call between plant managers. Dan was a case of a 'buddy' becoming a friend as we hung out together all summer, both at the plant and after work.

Our job on Neil's crew was to tag the many valves which made up the steam tracing system. There were numerous steam headers, each with 10 to 30 individual steam valves. The corresponding steam lines spread out from the header and went under the insulation of the process piping. Those steam lines then emerged from the insulation and ended up at a condensate header made up of individual steam traps and drain valves. The problem was that not all lines from a given steam header went to the same condensate header. It was very difficult to find the required isolation values when a steam leak was seen coming out from under a pipe's insulation. Very, very occasionally, there would be the remains of an old tag number on the valves. Dan and I thought it would make our task so much easier if we came up with our own new numbering system. Neil checked 'upstairs' with the engineering group and told us that we could use our own numbering scheme. At the time, this made sense because, when the plant was built, all the steam tracing lines were run in the field without engineering drawings.

So, off we went and what a great time we had! On rainy days, we would stay inside, making up new tags in an old construction hut which served as our home base for the summer. The rest of the time, we would pick a given condensate header and open all the un-tagged drain valves so that there was steam blowing all over the place. We would then close the individual steam header values until each drain valve stopped blowing. We could then tag the valves on both ends of the line. We had to remember to reopen all the steam valves so nothing would freeze on the next winter shutdown. We had free reign of the entire plant and were climbing all over the process piping, wherever and whenever we wanted. Dad made reference to the steam loss event and the scramble to find ladders to open all the steam tracing lines before they froze. I don't remember using a ladder that summer; Dan and I must have somehow found a way to climb to every header in the plant. By the end of the summer, we had everything tagged and documented in the form of a binder, listing all the valves on each header.

By working independently, it meant that Neil could concentrate on the steam line repair. By the end of the summer, the process area was almost free of steam leaks. This was a good thing as large blocks of ice would form around steam leaks in the winter, making a real mess. Neil took our binder upstairs at the end of the summer. The following summer, when the subject of the steam tracing came up, I asked what had happened to our binder. The story was that the engineer-in-charge looked at our valve numbering system, which did not match his numbering system, and threw our binder in the garbage. Obviously, this was not the same guy that Neil had checked with, at the being of the summer.

A special treat for Dan or I that summer, was to be asked to fill-in when the shift operating crew was short-handed. This involved working three hours of overtime at the end of the day, which entitled you to a free meal under the union contract. The meal was usually KFC, as this was the only fast-food place in Port Hawkesbury at that time. Overtime was paid at a time-and-a-half rate, and we were already being paid twice the provincial minimum wage. My two summers at the plant went a long way in getting me through my four year university degree without any significant student debt. That feat is near impossible today with the current costs of higher education and say, working at the local coffee shop for minimum wage.

Status at the plant was dictated by the colour of your hard hat. I proudly wore a red operations hat. The operators were well-respected, as they were the guys who looked after you if you were in trouble. Often, because of the hat, other workers would ask me where a specific piece of equipment was located, or voice a safety concern about leaking water or the smell of gas. Electricians wore green hats, mechanical maintainers wore grey, and labourers wore yellow. White hats were reserved for non-union staff from 'upstairs'. Finally, blue hats were for management. You would often hear, "Lookout, there are blue hats in the field."

One morning, early that first summer, the plant's 'Jesus Christ' gas alarm went off. It was not a man-down situation, but a general field evacuation because a gas leak, half-way up the second stage tower, had caught fire. Dan and I walked out of our field hut and saw the fire. We would have liked to stay to watch, but that was out of the question, as training dictated that we had to walk up the hill. On the way up to the administration building, I saw two blue hats coming down the hill. It was Dad and another manager. At home that night, still bristling a bit from not being able to watch the fire, I implied Dad was just watching too. He replied, "Who do you think OK'd the shutdown of the second stage tower?"

Outside of the control room, the lunchroom was the center of life at the plant, especially for the unionized personnel. The lunchroom would slowly fill in the morning until 8:00 am, when everyone would file into the back shop to start their day at work. It was just like a schoolyard emptying of kids as school started, except there was no bell. Again, at the end of the day, the room would fill slowly only to empty precisely at 4:30 pm as everyone filed out the plant door. Lord forbid that you work an extra minute. The lunchroom was also full for the morning, lunchtime and afternoon breaks. Work breaks where considered compulsory in the eyes of the union. Neil gave Dan and me a strange look when we said we did not want to walk up the hill in the rain for a break. The mid-morning and afternoon breaks were 15 minutes, but by the time you walked up the hill, took off your safety gear, took the break, restored your safety gear and walked back down the hill, at least 30 minutes was shot. And it would soon be time for lunch. It was a miracle that any work was got done at the plant.

Occasionally, you would see staff from upstairs in the lunchroom. One particular young woman, with her short skirt, would always turn a few heads, especially if she had to bend down to retrieve something from one of the vending machines which lined a wall of the lunchroom. Upon seeing this one day, Neil told us a story. Stories at the plant could capture your greatest successes, but could just as easily capture your worst moments. Neil's story revolved around a number of guys sitting at a lunchroom table, when that particular woman walked in. This was the early 70's, long before workplace sexual harassment was even in our vocabulary. One guy said, "Boy, would I love to do her."

To which a second guy at the table responded, "I do love to do her too, she is my wife!"

For all the animosity over the previous year's strike, I did not have any trouble during my two summers at the plant. This was probably because there were children of both union and non-union employees employed as summer students. It was also, in part, because I worked with operations, not maintenance, where the union support was strongest.

No trouble, but there is one story I have to tell. Neil, Dan and I were on break in the lunchroom early in the summer and I was waiting for the microwave to free up to heat water for my tea. Neil said there was a special hot-water tap, in the back shop, that people used for tea. With my mug and tea bag in hand, I headed to a wall in the back shop as directed by Neil. I could not see a tap, but there was a rather imposing pipe fitter standing there. I knew who he was, and assumed that he must have known who I was. We both stood there with neither of us saying a word, which seemed like forever. Then, with a mischievous grin on his face, he stepped aside, revealing the tap that I was looking for. It was not until I read this book, many years later, that I realized that this was the guy who had spat in Dad's face during the previous summer's strike.

During my second summer at the plant, I was assigned directly to operations on 'A' crew. Operators were now working on 12-hour shifts: 4 days on, 4 days off, 4 nights on and 4 days off. Dad told me A-shift was the most respected of the four shift crews. If there was a tricky or complicated procedure to be done, it was given to A-shift, if at all possible.

The shift supervisor was Wayne, who ran the plant from his office within the control room. The plant was on an extended shutdown when I first arrived. The shift supervisors had been temporarily taken off shift and stuck in a room together, with the task of re-writing the plant operational procedures. I am sure that this was considered a dry task for guys who were used to running a plant. Dad told me Wayne jokingly wrote a procedure called, *A Procedure for Writing Procedures*. The best line of the procedure was, "in event of an unexpected gas release, move away from your colleagues in the room."

With Wayne temporally on day shift, the day-to-day running of the plant fell to the shift foreman, George. The shift foreman, also based in the control room, was expected to go into the field regularly, so he needed a buddy, which was my job. As the foreman's buddy, I could also be called on to fill other positions on shift, in the case of an unexpected absence. The final person in the control room was the panel operator, Bob. Bob was very fond of this position as it was a clean, warm, year round assignment.

Then there was the DW operator who ran the distillation unit. The final operator action of the entire plant was for the DW operator to manually fill a steel barrel with a precise amount of heavy water. The barrel was sitting on a large weigh scale. This was accomplished using a gas station-like nozzle and hose extending from the final product tank. Our shift's DW operator was the same lackadaisical guy that Neil was worried about the previous summer. One backshift, I was sent to find him, as he was not responding to calls. I found him mopping up a large puddle of water on the floor by the filling station. I knew instantly what had happened, "Will they notice?" I asked.

"Maybe, it was quite a lot," he replied. By this time, Dad was running the Material Unaccounted For report. I am sure that there was a glitch in that week's report, but I never said a word to Dad.

A-shift's water treatment operator was John. John was one of the operators that climbed up to manually close the isolation valve during the B compressor fire, early in the plant's start-up. He was now enjoying the more solitary and sedentary life of a water treatment operator.

Before I continue with A-Shift's introduction, the shift change procedure has to be explained. The official shift change time was 7:30, both morning and evening. However, the incoming shift would start arriving any time after 7:00 o'clock. Once your replacement had arrived, and you handed off to him, you were free to leave for the day. Most people were gone long before 7:30.

Kevin was a Class I field operator, and unofficial lead field operator, since he was respected by everyone. Kevin knew his stuff and he always had an opinion on all aspects of the plant operation. Also, he was not shy in sharing that opinion, whether you were a foreman, supervisor or manager. Kevin was a bachelor, in his late twenties, and would sometimes burn the candle at both ends. On some days, I am sure he would head straight to the tavern after a 12 hour shift, have something to eat, and stay the evening.

Occasionally, Kevin would give me a lift to work as my home was on his way, just 5 minutes from the plant. If he was **not** out the night before, he would pick me up around 7:10am. If he had been out, he arrived at my place at 7:25am precisely. He would be slummed against the driver's door and just 'grunt' in response to my chipper morning greeting. He would not say another word until we got to the plant and he had had a couple of coffees.

Kevin's buddy was Ian. Ian was a short, funny guy, and second only to Neil in the story telling department. Ian did not mind playing second fiddle to Kevin, but Ian's claim to fame was that he was the guy who had finally convinced Neil to sit down on the back of the pickup truck and take some oxygen. This was a remarkable feat given that Ian was at least a foot shorter than Neil, who would have been flaying about as a result of the gassing. Ian's humor was subtle. One day a couple of guys were discussing how the train tracks coming into the plant were vandalized, in an effort to prevent an H_2S tanker delivery during the strike.

"Now, Now guys," said Ian in a fake admonishing voice, "You know the union's position on that. It was a late June frost that lifted those tracks". It is notable that the strike started on June 21st.

Jim and his buddy, whose name I can't recall, rounded out the second field operator team. The remainder of the shift included an electrician, an instrument tech, a pair of mechanical maintainers and a lab tech. So, that was A-shift. These 15 people ran the plant and responded to emergencies that occurred while they were on duty.

The two pairs of field operators worked out of a small hut, located at the bottom of the hill, close to the GS area on the admin side of the plant. The hut would, of course, be a welcome refuge from the winter weather, but even in the summer, it was a social place and the center of field activities for the plant. It was in that hut, where I heard many of those great plant stories. Sleeping on shift was not allowed of course; however, if things were quiet on backshift, the stories would stop and you could close your eyes, put your feet up on the desk and quietly reflect on things in your life.

In early May, things were pretty relaxed on shift as there was not a lot for operations to do when the plant was shut down. All the H_2S gas was back in the H_2S storage area, so the main GS area was gas-free. Even some towers had been opened up maintenance work. So the last thing any of us expected was a man-down gas alarm.

I was filling in for Jim's buddy, who was off that day. There was a requirement that at least one pair of operators be in the field at all times. So, with Keven and Ian up in the control room, it was Jim and I who were out in the field. We were at one end of the GS unit when the alarm went off. The panel operator would have announced the location of the man-down, both over the PA system and over the operator radios. As I said, things had gotten very relaxed, and Jim had not yet obtained a replacement for his broken radio. Jim and I ran to the nearest rescue station. My wish had come true; no slow walk up to hill for me on this alarm. The rescue station contains two pairs of Scott breathing apparatus and an oxygen respirator. Jim had his SCBA on before me, of course, and took off running. I followed as soon as I could, but I was lagging behind him. Like Dad said, just wearing an SCBA was stress enough, and we had not even put our masks on yet. We headed to the H_2S storage area at the other end of the plant. By the time Jim got to the other end of the plant, he could see there was nobody there. He turned around and ran back to me and asked, "Did you hear where the alarm was?" I had not. He then gave me the oxygen and took off running back to the operator's hut for its telephone. I was now even slower, carrying the oxygen, and only got to the hut as Jim came running out again and stated, "Third level tower catwalk." Then he took off again.

"Oh shit," I thought, as I knew that use of the elevator was not allowed during gas-alarms. Personnel on the catwalks, during a gas alarm, had to stay in place so as not to risk coming down into gas. I had already run the equivalent of once around the entire GS area, carrying an SCBA on my back. I thought that I would need the oxygen myself if I had to run up those stairs! I caught up with Jim at the base of the towers, as he was getting into the elevator, thank god. On the way up, we put on our breathing masks and walked out onto the catwalk. Talk about being late for a party; the catwalk was packed with people who had been working inside the towers. We were the only ones wearing masks. Somehow, Kevin and Ian were already there, quite remarkable given they were in the control room when the alarm sounded. They had already determined it was a false alarm. Reportedly a wire shorted in the red gas alarm button on the catwalk. It was more likely that someone flipped the switch for fun, just like a kid pulling a school fire alarm.

Later, in the lunchroom, I was talking to a summer student who was working as a tower safety monitor. On hearing the alarm, he did as he was instructed and flashed the lights inside the tower. This was the evacuation signal for the workers inside. He then heard, "Leave the f***ing lights alone!"

So, he stuck his head into the open manhole and yelled, "Gas!" He said that emptied the tower quickly enough. When I got home that night, I resolved to start jogging to get in better shape, an activity which I was to continue for the rest of my time at university.

Activity on shift was picking up as the plant start-up drew closer. Late one afternoon, I had accompanied John, in the shift pickup truck, to run something down to the operators in the field. We were all sitting around the hut chatting when we heard a series of loud bangs from the GS area. The control room called and asked what that noise was, as they had heard it as well. It was getting louder, as we all took off, looking for the source. It was soon determined to be a 'water hammer' in the steam line from the power plant next door. This water hammer was caused by steam hitting cold standing water in the line. The water had expanded rapidly and caused the line to shake violently. I followed John, under the plant fence, as he looked for drain valves along the line. This would both, remove the standing water, and reduce the steam pressure in the line. I was running next to the line when the loudest water hammer hit, the force of which lifted a couple hundred foot section of this 48 inch diameter steam line at least a foot off of its support! The hammering soon subsided as the steam pressure was reduced.

Before long, we were back at the hut discussing the event. Even with the event less than an hour old, the story had started to take on a life of its own, with Kevin saying he had 'jumped' the fence. I believe it was only John and I who were outside the fence that day. This only confirmed my suspicion of some exaggeration in other stories I had heard that summer.

When I got home that night, Dad said the problem was caused by the 4:00 pm shift change at the power plant. The previous shift had only cracked the steam line valve to slowly warm-up the line. The next shift assumed the line was ready and put full pressure to the line. The steam line had to be X-rayed before it could be put back in-service.

In this book, Dad referenced a strike at the power plant that summer, but stated that he thought that the professional staff personnel had seemed to be doing a good job. Either, Dad forgot this incident, or the strike had not yet started.

The plant start-up continued and Wayne was back on duty as shift supervisor. It was then that the highlight of my short 'operator' career occurred. George took me up to the top level catwalk, gave me a set of earmuffs, a pipe wrench and, pointing to a valve, said, "Open that vent valve there as much as you can until the noise gets too much." The vent valve was at the top of the second stage return gas line, the highest point of the tower. To reach it, you had to climb from the top catwalk up to smaller platform, and then up an enclosed metal ladder. Normally, that high up, you would hear wind noise, but with my earmuffs on, it was eerily quiet. But, not for long! There was an ear-piercing sound as I opened the valve and 150 psi steam came out; it would have been heard all over the plant. It was a 3 inch valve, a lot bigger than any steam tracing valve I had opened the previous summer.

At home that night, Dad asked me, "Do you know they are getting ready to put the second stage tower back in service?"

"Yes", I said proudly, "I was the one who vented the tower."

With all the towers now closed up, the next major start-up milestone was putting the H_2S gas back in the GS unit. With this activity pending, George announced early one night shift, that it would be a good time for a man-down practice drill. Sure enough, George and I were walking around the unit by ourselves at about 3 am when he told me to lie down and not move. Off he ran. The

'Jesus Christ' alarm sounded. Four guys appeared in SCBA and put an oxygen mask on my face. They then loaded me into the back of the ambulance and I was driven up the hill. By the time Wayne met me at the administration building, I was almost a sleep. After all, I was laying down on a comfortable gurney and it was still the middle of the night. At the post-drill briefing, Ian asked me what I had felt. Even though I had stretched the buddy rules a bit the previous summer with Dan, I said, "I have never felt as alone as when George ran away."

Ian laughed, "I knew it. I knew it. Everyone says that."

The next evening shift, H_2S gas was returned to the GS unit, with no problems except the slight smell of gas during the shift. Again, it was another one of those tricky tasks successfully carried out by A-shift.

That summer I had an infection in a wisdom tooth and the dentist said it should come out. Mum picked me up at the plant mid-morning and drove me to the dentist. After the extraction, but still in the dental chair, the dental assistant asked how I was doing. I said fine and she accompanied me to the reception area where I promptly passed out. The dentist came out and said I should take it easy for the rest of the day. Dad must have explained what happened to the shift supervisor, so as to account for my absence for the remainder of the shift. I knew this because, the next day at work, Ian had nicknamed me, 'Wilting Ray'

During a set of night shifts some time later, George and I were heading out for our first excursion of the shift. George handed me a basket full of plastic sample bottles, which we were to be taken down to the field operators for their routine process sampling. George got distracted by something and I was standing by myself looking out of the control room window. I looked at the sample bottles and knew they contained 'sour' water because of the characteristic dirty black coloring. I wondered just how bad it would smell. The bottles were small, only slightly bigger than my hand. I cracked one open, but I did not even get it anywhere near my nose. The smell hit me like a ton of bricks and my head started to spin. I thrust the bottle away from me, and luckily, I was able to get the top back on at the same time. The combination of my head recoiling back and my arm moving the bottle away meant I almost lost my balance. I locked my knees and just stood there until the dizziness passed. I did not feel normal again until George and I were outside walking around. It was a stupid and potentially dangerous thing to do. I am not sure what would have happened if I had dropped that open bottle. At the very least, it would have made great story. I can just hear them now, "Did you ever hear the story of Wilting Ray gassing himself in the control room…"

Dad had lots of opportunities to go up the flare tower. The flare tower was almost twice as high as the top tower catwalk. I almost had my chance to go up; on one night shift, there was an issue with the propane igniters at the top of the tower. George had me pressing the igniter button on the control room panel, which was the only time I was ever allowed to touch anything on the panel, while he used binoculars to check for a flame. By morning, when it was light,

George and I were down in the field with Kevin and Ian discussing the flare ignitor problem. Then Kevin said to George, "I'll go up. Ray will come with me," and then, as an afterthought, he turned to me and said, "You would come up with me, right?"

Kevin had me cased correctly, as I replied, "Sure." For whatever reason, George nixed the excursion that morning and I never got to go up the flare tower.

Towards the end of the summer, I put in my notice as I was returning to university. I was asked if I could stay a bit longer to cover an upcoming vacation, but it was too late in September, so I had to refuse. If I had stayed, I would have been there for the TS561 tank explosion as A-shift was on duty that fateful morning.

In my final days, George announced some changes to A-shift when we were down in the hut. Kevin was to be moved to the control room as panel operator and Bob would take Kevin's place in the field. Kevin laughed, "Bob won't like that. They don't call him the 'Hollywood' operator for nothing. He can work an entire shift and not get his coveralls dirty."

Later, when I was talking to Bob, he said, "I don't think someone should be moved if they are doing a good job." However, it was not about Bob. My guess is that it was about grooming Kevin for possible promotion to shift foreman and supervisor. A couple of days later, at the start of shift, I noticed Bob walking down to the field in a clean set of coveralls.

On my last day, George sent me to the company store to get a slip to say that I had returned everything that had been issued to me. At the store wicket, I said that all I had been issued was my hard hat and safety glasses, but that I needed them for the balance of my shift, which did not end till after the store wicket closed. The guy said not to worry as he would be throwing them in the garbage anyway, because they were regarded as used personal safety equipment. So, at the end my shift, I walked out of the plant for the last time, proudly wearing my red hard hat. Today, that hard hat still hangs in my basement, just in case I need it.

Dad spearheaded the organization of a Port Hawkesbury heavy water plant reunion in 1994, 20 years after full production. By this time, the towers were gone and the plant's GS area had been levelled, but that did not matter. Mum and Dad came up from California, along with many others who came from all over North America. There was an evening social event at a local hotel – a social event where nobody nearly drowned or got food poisoning. Dad enjoyed seeing so many former GE employees, who had been with him during those challenging years. I went along, as a former employee, and totally enjoyed myself as well. Quite a few of A-shift showed up, including Kevin, who travelled back from his job at the oil sands in Alberta.

Of course, Neil, now living the life of a retired Cape Bretoner, still had lots of stories to tell. One I had not heard before: AECL had taken over the plant from CGE early in my last summer there. At that time, the union and AECL had entered contract negotiations, which were successfully concluded sometime in the fall, without a strike. According to Neil, the negotiations were just finishing up when the union brought up the issue of back pay for former employees. This affected primarily the summer students, as they had all gone back to school by then. AECL said "No."

Neil said the union thought to themselves, "Oh well, no big deal, we tried." Since this was the last item on the union's list, they stood up to leave.

Then AECL, thinking the union was walking out on the negotiations, said, "OK, OK... we'll pay the back pay." I thought Neil's story was a little far-fetched, but then I did receive a $350 cheque in the mail from AECL around Christmas that year

It was several years after I had graduated from university, and only after I had experienced my own 'start-up' trials and tribulations during the commissioning at the Point Lepreau Nuclear Power Station, that I fully understood the exhilaration and fulfillment that Dad had felt with his challenging work at the heavy water plant. That experience allowed me to fully appreciate what Dad had once told me, "If you are lucky, a once-in-a-lifetime job like that comes along..."

Made in the USA
Las Vegas, NV
05 March 2023

68558321R00157